Practical
Intuition™
FOR SUCCESS

Also by Laura Day

Practical Intuition™

Practical Intuition™
FOR SUCCESS

A STEP-BY-STEP PROGRAM TO
INCREASE YOUR WEALTH TODAY

~~~

LAURA DAY

HarperPerennial
A Division of HarperCollinsPublishers

HarperCollins books may be purchased for educational, business, or sales promotional use. For information please write: Special Markets Department, HarperCollins Publishers, Inc., 10 East 53rd Street, New York, NY 10022.

First HarperPerennial edition published 1999.

Designed by Helene Wald Berinsky

The Library of Congress has catalogued the hardcover edition as follows:

Day, Laura.
  Practical intuition for success : a step-by-step program to increase your wealth today / Laura Day.
     p.   cm.
  ISBN 0-06-017576-1
  1. Success. 2. Intuition. I. Title.
BJ1611.2.D39   1997
332.024'01—dc21   97-22785

ISBN 0-06-093022-5 (pbk.)

  01 02 03 ❖/RRD 10 9 8 7 6 5 4 3

CONTENTS

FOREWORD

Intuition is not a dirty word, but too many successful people are afraid to acknowledge its power and value.

The very successful publisher (and publishing books requires great intuition) who is also an incredibly successful gambler brags about his ability to call the next roll of the dice and goes ballistic when someone even whispers "intuition."

And the very successful commodities trader who was also a champion squash player (a sport that benefits substantially from intuition) walked out of a small dinner party when the discussion turned to intuition.

Actually, the driving force in America is intuition—untamed intuition. Let's buy this company. Let's put a store in this location. Let's develop this new product.

The concept may come intuitively, but then it is very important to apply diligent consequential thinking. What are the consequences of the planned action, and what are the consequences of those consequences?

In our affluent society with huge markets, just about anything goes. America may indeed be wealthy enough to be profligate, but by applying our intuition intelligently and filtering the ideas carefully, we can make better use of our many assets.

Women certainly have. Just a little more than twenty years ago, there was not a significant number of women in the workforce nor in positions of management. They have gone on to do amazing things in the business world. And it all happened so fast. In the occupations that I deal with, women have risen to the same levels as men.

How did that happen? Women's intuition and hard work! They were famous for intuition well before they arrived in the workforce. It was essential for their existence. Who was safe to be with? Which street was safe to walk? They use their intuition and intelligence to select the father of their children, though "the system" is making it harder and harder.

Tuning into our intuition works in many ways. In a contentious interview in the *Wall Street Journal* years ago, the great Peter Drucker was asked why he talked so much. His beautiful and simple answer—because I learn so much when I talk aloud. Talking is one of Peter's ways of tuning into his intuition.

Isn't that what happens when we talk to a psychiatrist? Or a management consultant? The answers are so often inside of us. We just have to let them out. It is exciting to carefully examine those thoughts and then apply intuition to the product of the analysis of our earlier intuition.

Many years ago, before I understood what intuition or feelings really were, a woman who worked for me came into my office to disagree with a position I had taken earlier. She said, "I know you are wrong because I feel it in my whole body."

I learned a lot from that conversation. I now use that "body feeling" in much of what I do . . . as I edit articles . . . write headlines, etc.

Martin Kessler, the famous editor of Basic Books, taught me to challenge everything with two simple questions: Is it genuine? Is it baloney? Those questions work remarkably well. I use them regularly. Check your premise, think it through, and check your intuition. Write it down. Break it down into parts to examine it closely.

Many years ago, the innovative entrepreneur Bob Schwartz told Eric Utne about the difficulty he was having making some decisions. Eric told Bob to ask himself how each of the options felt to him. If they feel good—great. If they don't feel good, beware. I have tried it, and it works much of the time. Here, too, it is important to get as much information as you can and then double-check.

Einstein was reported to have said that we only use 2 percent to 10 percent of our ability. With intuition, it is possible to go far beyond that. Use intuition as an energizing force. It can surely help you operate much more effectively. To quote Teddy Roosevelt, "I am just an average person who works much harder than the average person."

Laura lays it all out here. Intuition is a system. It is much more than a feeling, much more than an idea. And it works.

MARTIN EDELSTON

PREFACE

Over the course of the last decade, I have consulted with different kinds of individuals, corporations, and institutions. I was brought in, usually, at times of change or crisis, and often asked to evaluate in detail one small part of the operation. I would see snatches of a company's operations: marketing or collections or customer service or whatever.

Consulting in this manner, I realized that I was being asked to evaluate isolated symptoms rather than the cause of problems at their most fundamental level. By addressing the individual or company as a whole, we could not only solve the particular difficulty efficiently but also simultaneously eliminate a host of other seemingly unrelated problems. I also met with individuals who were struggling in business because they were simply, for a variety of reasons, on the wrong path.

I longed for the opportunity to address the system of a company or individual as a whole. My life provided that opportunity. After my son was born, I encountered my own business crisis. Not only was my previous financial support gone, but at the same time I was struck by an unrelated and crushing expense.

I turned to my own intuition and in so doing reopened a clear dialogue with myself and every aspect of my environment. I experienced firsthand how doing something of value to me could create something valuable, marketable, and integral for others. In allowing my intuition to restore my integrity, I improved my own personal success in every area of my life.

I wrote this book to share with you a perspective as well as a methodology for improving your own personal success.

ACKNOWLEDGMENTS

I was sitting one evening at Susan and Victor Niederhoffer's dinner table on one of our regular weekend visits to their home. Victor, who reads a passage from a great work at each meal, had chosen an especially "battle intensive" but nonetheless literary selection in deference to my young son's interests. Their many daughters were also listening raptly—just kidding, kids!—and I was struck by the good fortune of our family— Samson, Adam, and I—to be included in theirs.

I am blessed with good friends and would like to thank some of them on this page.

Let me start with Mr. William Beslow, whose integrity and wisdom (not to mention hard work) has given me the shelter to thrive. Thank you.

Melanie Jackson, my agent, thank you for your faith, your brilliance, and for never "doing lunch" where we can't bring our kids.

Joëlle Delbourgo, my editor, for being such a good intuitive that I have never had to finish a sentence, and for your inspired editing and coaching.

Marty Edelston, for your friendship and generosity of deed and spirit.

Carol de Fritsch, for your wise counsel (every morning at seven).

Christine Henrich, for your wise counsel (not before noon but always after midnight).

Demi Moore, my mother/daughter/sister, for sharing so open-heartedly with me and my family.

Jean Althshuler Fasciano and Renee Glichlich, my models for courage and determination.

My godsons, Gabriel and Jeremy Glissen-Brown, who blessed me with their choice.

My goddaughter, Eva LaGambina, and her brother Giulio, for showing me what to expect, and the newly arrived Valerio for showing them.

My Italian family, LaGambina, Pino, Piero, Leyla, Stephania, Nonna, and *la bella* Caterina, for two decades of friendship.

My Merlin, Bruno dell Rosso, for creating knowledge from mysteries.

Alice Micheals, Emma Torres, Helen Bransford, and Suzzanne Maas, for making me feel like I was just another lady having tea when my hair was standing on end and my shoes were on the wrong feet.

My brilliant siblings (in order of age), Martha, Alexander, and Sarah; if you weren't related to me I would have had to find you.

My delicious nephews (in order of age), Zachary, Carson, and Ori. Our family's pride and joy (along with cousin Samson), who prove that the wheel can be improved.

My father, Dr. David L. Globus, for being "the surviving parent," teaching me the phrase "it's blood over the dam," and knowing when it's time to be a friend to your children.

Adam Robinson, I am so lucky to know you and live in your love. I love you.

Samson, for being such a fine human being and for sharing your computer with me.

For all of you, and you know who you are, who cared so deeply about Samson that he resembles each of you in some important way. This is the greatest gift of all.

Thank you.

INTRODUCTION

No problem can be solved from the same consciousness that created it. We must learn to see the world anew.

—ALBERT EINSTEIN

THIS BOOK IS YOUR WEALTH-CREATING ROAD MAP

If you're reading this book, I assume you want to be more profitable by increasing your salary or your net worth. But I also assume that you want to be working effectively and efficiently at something that gives you satisfaction and adds to your quality of life.

So this book answers the following question: How can I increase my wealth by being who I am? That may sound like a tall order. After all, most people would be happy simply making more money. But personal satisfaction? Isn't that expecting too much?

No, it's not. It's easy to be profitable by being yourself. What's hard is being profitable trying to be someone you're not.

To succeed in business is not a matter of "beating the competition." It's simply a matter of being who you are. And that's true for corporations as well as individuals.

You have something unique to offer the job market. You also have a unique business inside you, if that's the way you choose to go. This book will give you a step-by-step plan for realizing either ambition, and in so doing increasing your wealth. All it takes is one good interaction with the right person, one insight into an unmet need in your market.

With the very first chapter, you'll learn techniques you can put into operation immediately. Today. Right now.

YOU ALREADY HAVE EVERYTHING YOU NEED

I won't show you how to change yourself or change your market. Rather, I'll show you how to choose from the skills and knowledge and experience you already have, and put those resources to work in a way that's more effective. In short, this book will show you how to use more of yourself.

DO ANY OF THESE SITUATIONS SOUND FAMILIAR?

"I don't understand what I'm missing. I read stories of people who start businesses based on the most simple and obvious ideas—and make fortunes overnight. Why can't I do something like that?"

"I manage a division whose performance has been slipping each quarter. We've called in consultants and tried all the latest management fads, but nothing seems to work. What are we doing wrong?"

"I'm the head of a major company whose productivity, quality control, and revenues have all been increasing, but whose market share and stock price have been steadily eroding. How can I turn this around?"

"I have all my retirement funds invested in the stock market. Although my portfolio has done well over the past decade, I'm concerned about the recent volatility in the market. Is the bull market over or should I 'take my profits' and invest them more safely in money market funds?"

"I meet people in my industry who not only have a college degree but a master's (and sometimes more). My background just doesn't measure up. I don't have the same advantages, the same resources, even the same ambition and stick-to-itiveness."

"I've done my best in my current job. But even though I've given it my all, I don't seem to get very far. My company just hired someone from the outside to fill a position I've always had my eye on. And to add insult to injury, this person had less experience and fewer qualifications. Why can't I get ahead?"

"I have so many great ideas every day, but I can't seem to get it together to act on them. The pieces just get lost, and then a year later I end up seeing someone else get it together and make it a success. It's the same idea, and it's never even executed as well as I could have done it."

"I'm successful but it feels like a constant struggle to stay that way. When do I get to sit back and enjoy what I've accomplished? There is so little pleasure in the taking because it's so exhausting just keeping up."

"I've been successful for years, but recently things began to unravel. My old tricks aren't working anymore. I'm almost afraid to act because everything I do turns out wrong."

"By most people's standards I'm successful—even incredibly so—but I'm bored. I just don't like my old job anymore, but I can't give it up because my lifestyle depends on it."

"I'm just entering the workforce and I have no idea what I want to do 'with the rest of my life.' There are so many possibilities and I just don't know which one to choose. I'm afraid to make a mistake. I want to do a million things and I feel pulled in so many different directions."

"My industry is changing so rapidly that my career, much less my company or my job, may not exist five years from now. What do I do next?"

"I've always thought of starting a business, but I couldn't figure out what mine is. And even if I could, who has the time or money to carry it out?"

"I need a bolt of lightning! I know I need to improve my professional skills, but a new course of study? Forget it! I have so many things on my plate already, I don't see how I can work any harder than I already am. And an MBA? You must be kidding. I can't afford to take the time off."

What Are You Sacrificing?

The way modern business and life is structured, most of us feel that we have no choice but to conform to the work world without considering our own needs or really even those of the marketplace.

Consider the job-seeker scanning the want ads. He sees an offer in his field that lists qualifications A, B, and C. So he responds to the company with a cover letter trying to embellish his background and experience to match those precise qualifications in that precise order. It doesn't even dawn on him that he might be truly superb at something else—a skill or expertise that the company is *really* looking for—if only he knew how to get the important information about that company that would enable him to market himself in a compelling way.

We've all been in this position, and sooner or later we find a job. But because we haven't considered either our own needs or those of our market and business world—because, in short, we've compromised our integrity—we find ourselves continually struggling. Deep down we sense this, but we think that the solution is to offer as much as we can as brilliantly as we can. And so we waste still more time and energy offering only a small part of ourselves.

The real problem is that we're trying to be someone we're not, and this compromise with our integrity takes a toll not only on our careers but on our lives.

It Doesn't Have to Be This Way

While you can be successful without considering your personal integrity as well as that of your market, you won't be operating effectively and efficiently—and probably not for long.

I'm reminded of the sport of swimming, in which the greatest advances in the past twenty years have come not from increasing the strength or propulsive force of athletes, but rather from dramatic increases in streamlining. In other words, swimmers have learned that the most effective way to increase their speed is to lessen or remove hindrances rather than to try harder or more furiously.

I say this because no matter how hard you try, until you've removed your external—and internal—hindrances, true success and fulfillment will continue to elude you. What's getting in your way may be more a matter of understanding yourself and your needs than of understanding the business world.

Intuition will enable you to gain these insights. More important, through intuition you'll put more of yourself, and use more of yourself, in business. In turn, you'll learn to use business to enliven yourself.

You Can Have It All: Finding Your Integrity

Integrity means finding an unobstructed path to agreement, acceptance, and success.

Integrity is knowing what you love to do and have to give as well as what the market needs.

Integrity is knowing how to involve and inspire people and resources who can express that idea or product or service as completely as possible.

Integrity is knowing how to present what you're offering so that it is useful, inspiring, and meaningful to the people and companies who make up your market.

Finally, integrity is about finding a way for all of these things to work together. It's about not compromising or selling out, but instead finding the *balance point* between what you have to offer and what your market desires.

If you are offering a product or a service valued by your market, you've achieved integrity with your market. If you're offering something not valued by your market, you have no integrity with your market (though you may, of course, have integrity with another market).

Not only *can* you have it all, but if you want to achieve true success and fulfillment, you *must*.

BUSINESS 101

Economics can be boiled down to two words: supply and demand. Business pretty much comes down to the same thing, though management consultants would have us believe it's a complex enterprise: what you have to offer the marketplace and what the marketplace wants.

This is true whether you're looking for your first job, thinking about starting a business, or running a multinational conglomerate. The first-time job-hunter offers his or her skills to companies that want those skills. The would-be entrepreneur dreams of offering a product or service to individuals or companies who want it. The multinational conglomerate is already doing that on a global scale.

The first step is always the same: Take the time to ask what this company (or person, or market) wants and needs. This may sound like an obvious starting point, but the problem is that we *think* we know what the company needs.

You see, business really comes down to *values*, *perceptions*, and *communication*.

Values are what we feel are important for our survival. They include both what is being offered and what the marketplace wants. More specifically, values are what you are offering and what your market wants.

Perceptions are both yours—how you perceive your market—and how your market perceives you.

Communication is staying in touch with your market and its values. You must understand your market to put forth your product or service so that it feels integral, so your market believes it has value. Without constant communication, you won't be able to stay in touch with how your market is growing and how its values are changing, with how you can improve what you're offering and make it more responsive to your market's changing needs.

This is where intuition comes in.

WHY INTUITION IS CRITICAL TO BUSINESS SUCCESS

Business schools and MBAs may forget this, but it's important to remember that whatever you're selling—your skills as an employee or your products and services as a company—you're selling to human beings; to mammals, not computers. Your market is a living, breathing entity with a subtle, intangible, ever-changing pulse. So while focus groups and spreadsheets and analysis have their place, the only truly effective way to figure out what your market values are is by adding intuition to the process.

Intuition is a way of receiving information about your environment that is not directly evident either to your senses or to your reasoning mind. It's knowing how to perceive a market so that you can create your most profitable response given the skills, talents, and experience that you have to offer. It's not that we need to know more by accumulating mountains and mountains of data, but rather that we need to know where to focus our attention.

Archimedes said that with a fixed point and a long enough lever, he could move the earth. Your intuition is like a lever that focuses your attention so that you know what you need to know, without knowing so much that your attention and efforts get scattered.

HOW YOU CAN USE INTUITION

Intuition is about answering questions. It can be used in business in the following ways:

- **to gather information** (What strategy is our competitor planning?)
- **to solve problems** (What is the best way to resolve the budget dispute?)
- **to spot opportunities** (What new markets for my company's products will develop in the next year?)
- **to create** (What should I name my new company?)

- **to decide** (What will convince my boss to give me a raise?)
- **to plan** (What is the best way to expand our company's market share?)
- **to evaluate** (Which of these job offers should I take?)
- **to predict** (What will the Dow Jones average be in six months?)
- **to time** (When will be the best time to buy a house?)

TWO ORDINARY INDIVIDUALS WHO FOLLOWED THEIR GUT TO EXTRAORDINARY SUCCESS

To show you how intuition can guide you to a career rooted in your integrity, I've selected two inspiring stories: one about a job-hunter, the other about an entrepreneur. Each followed a hunch, and within a year had achieved incredible success.

And if they can do it . . .

~~~~~~

AN INTUITIVE TALE
STARTING A BUSINESS

In 1995, Dineh Mohajer was a twenty-two-year-old premed student at the University of Southern California when—out of the blue—she decided to launch a cosmetics company.

Did Dineh have any experience in this field? No.

Did she have a business plan? No.

Did she even conduct market research to see whether there was a market for a new line of cosmetics? No.

Yet by following her gut she became an overnight success and within a year she had built a multimillion-dollar business.

How did she do it? By following her instincts. Dineh hated the typical berry-berry reds and pinks of traditional nail polish. Why, she wondered, couldn't nail polish come in pastels to match California's fashion sensibility? So one day she mixed a bit of blue dye with white nail polish and dabbed it on her nails. Her friends asked her where they could get some.

Testing the waters, she prepared four more bottles that day and convinced a popular boutique to take them on consignment.

They sold out in less than an hour, and the boutique asked Dineh for two hundred more.

She was in business. Running out to cosmetics stores to buy up all the white polish she could find, she decided to add three more colors: pale yellow, violet, and green. She also came up with a name: Hard Candy.

Dineh proved to be a natural entrepreneur with a knack for promotion. She coined provocatively catchy names for the colors: Dork, Sissy, Frigid, and Trailer Trash. She also designed bottles that reinforced the rebellious image, placing plastic trinkets on each bottle cap.

Dineh was on a roll. No sooner had these colors landed on the shelves than they were on the hands of fashion-forward Hollywood celebrities. The hot, not-yet-twenty-something actress Alicia Silverstone wore Hard Candy nail polish on the David Letterman show. *Elle* magazine raved about it. And MTV's *House of Style* hyped the line of nail polish in a segment.

Dineh decided it was time to recruit Hard Candy's first two employees: her sister Pooneh, a lawyer, and her boyfriend, Benjamin Einstein, a musician. She then borrowed fifty thousand dollars from her parents and set up shop in her campus apartment. *Forbes* magazine reports that "pastel polish stuck like chewing gum to her living room floor and overflowed from the bathroom and kitchen basins."

Before long Dineh's crew was producing tens of thousands of bottles of Hard Candy nail polish every month. Demand was so strong that she was able to charge her customers, Southern California's most fashionable boutiques, more than twice what her competitors were able to command.

The business quickly outgrew her cramped apartment, and she was soon looking for office space. The fledgling enterprise was almost undone by its heady growth, however, and Dineh realized that if she were going to survive she needed inventory systems, financial controls, and experienced management.

Enlisting an executive recruiter, she used her intuition (and good sense) to sign on William Botts, a sixty-one-year-old former nuclear engineer, as Hard Candy's chief executive officer. An entrepreneur himself, Botts had turned around a number of small start-up companies, including one in the cosmetics field.

Dineh ended up with a CEO who knew her business and knew how to keep it running. At the end of 1996, its first full year in business, Dineh Mohajer's company reported $10 million in sales and a pretax profit of $2.5 million. Freed now to focus on the more creative aspects, Hard Candy's founder plunged ahead. She has since expanded her cosmetics beyond nail polish to include lipstick, eye shadow, and mascara. Ever the trendsetter, Dineh recently unveiled a line of nail polish for men.

She must be doing something right. Sales in her second year were double those of the previous year, and Dineh is contemplating an initial public offering in another year or two.

Invited to speak at the Yale Business and Economic Forum in February 1997, she had two pieces of advice for aspiring entrepreneurs: "Don't be afraid to delegate," she said, and "go with your gut!"

AN INTUITIVE TALE
CREATING A JOB

Forty years before Dineh Mohajer launched Hard Candy, Eppie Lederer was a housewife who one day found herself with nothing to do. Despite her complete lack of work experience of any kind, she talked her way into one of the most famous syndicated features in American journalism.

It was the mid-1950s. Eppie and her family moved to Chicago from Eau Claire, Wisconsin. She did not need to support her family; her husband was a successful executive who frequently traveled. But now that her teenager was in school most of the time, Eppie had a lot of time on her hands.

She wanted to work. But doing what? She had never worked before and had no idea "what she wanted to do." One day she was reading the *Chicago Sun-Times* when her attention was grabbed by a new feature.

It was an advice column by Ann Landers, and Eppie was fascinated. Each and every letter to Ann Landers was to receive a personal reply from the columnist, whether or not it appeared in the paper.

It occurred to her in a flash that Ann Landers would be overwhelmed with correspondents and would certainly need an assistant. On the spur of the moment, she called the *Sun-Times* to speak with Will Munnecke, an executive she knew at the paper, to see whether such a position existed.

Munnecke told her that as chance would have it, Ruth Crowley (a.k.a. Ann Landers) had just passed away. Seizing the opportunity, Eppie instantly switched gears. Rather than being "Ann Landers's" assistant, she proposed that she become the columnist.

Munnecke tactfully pointed out that Eppie lacked journalistic skills, while the former columnist had been a reporter as well as a nurse. Undaunted, Eppie asked how the new columnist would be chosen.

Munnecke told her that to ensure objectivity, the new columnist would be selected in a blind competition among twenty-one experienced journalists who would be asked to submit sample columns in response to actual letters from readers. Eppie proposed that she be allowed to enter the monthlong contest.

Munnecke, perhaps patronizing his friend's wife, relented. When the final results were tallied, Eppie had won the competition. And despite the misgivings the newspaper's executives had about handing over the column to someone "with no experience," Eppie became Crowley's successor. And for nearly four decades, Eppie Lederer has been the Ann Landers we've all known.

━━━━━

THE LESSONS

Despite the generation gap and their different paths, both Lederer and Mohajer share a number of common attributes.

Each lacked any qualifications or experience that might have helped in her chosen path. Indeed, each chose to act on her instincts despite many obvious "logical" objections.

Each created a situation in keeping with her true desires rather than responding to what was being offered.

And each experienced immediate success in the marketplace.

What's more, Lederer and Mohajer pursued their dreams by following the same game plan: using intuition to sense what the marketplace wanted while combining that with what each had to offer.

CREATING YOUR PERSONAL WEALTH PLAN: THE TEN QUESTIONS YOU MUST ANSWER

Every successful corporation has a mission statement that describes why it's in business. This statement states precisely the corporation's market or markets, what needs of those markets it's serving, and how it expects to satisfy those needs.

To increase your wealth most effectively, you, too, must have a personal mission statement. To do this is simply a matter of answering ten questions:

QUESTION 1: What is my business world? (It's bigger than you think.)

QUESTION 2: What does this person—or company, or market—want? (Careful: They might not even know.)

QUESTION 3: What do *I* want (you can and should have it all) and have to offer in exchange? (It's always more than you think.)

QUESTION 4: What is the best fit between my needs and the market's? (There's always a creative solution to achieving integrity: the *balance point* where everyone wins.)

QUESTION 5: What steps must I take to achieve this goal? (You can plan for tomorrow today.)

QUESTION 6: How can I best present myself and what I am offering? (To sell your product, service, or skill, you must "speak" in a language your market understands and responds to.)

QUESTION 7: How can I get others to help me? (You must understand and satisfy their needs, too.)

QUESTION 8: How can I prevent others from interfering? (Again, you must consider their needs.)

QUESTION 9: How can I anticipate and overcome obstacles? (It's possible to solve problems before they arise.)

QUESTION 10: How can I stay ahead of my market to respond to changing needs and opportunities? (Success in the marketplace is not a static thing.)

We'll devote a chapter to answering each of these questions. By the end of this book, you will have a step-by-step road map you can follow to increase your wealth.

INTUITION AND INTEGRITY IN THE CORPORATE AND INVESTING WORLDS

Everything we've discussed so far about the need to balance your needs with those of the market applies to companies, too. So along the way we'll examine companies that have thrived by maintaining their integrity—the Disney Corporation, for example—and those that have lost touch with the needs of their marketplace, such as the Apple Computer Corporation.

You will also see how the concepts of market needs and integrity can be profitably applied in the investing world. Our concern here is not selling yourself or your company to the market, but rather knowing how to keep yourself focused so that you can accurately perceive the market and respond to it proactively and effectively.

HOW TO STAY ONE STEP AHEAD OF YOUR MARKET

By adding intuition and integrity to your business life, you will know your market as well as you know yourself. You'll develop such an intimate sense of your market that you'll actually be able to predict what it will want—or, in the case of the stock market, what it will do—well before the changes become "obvious" to everyone else.

EVERYTHING IN THIS BOOK WAS WRITTEN FOR YOU

Each chapter in this book will help you respond to your situations more effectively. This book is written in plain language, with simple exercises all mapped out with everything you need to do to transform your working life.

Even if you've never worked in a company before, even if you have no product in mind, even if you don't know what you want to do "with the rest of your life," there are ways you can adapt each lesson, each exercise, and each anecdote to your situation. If you're reading this book because you're looking for a job, for example, what I have to say on starting a business may open new perspectives and vistas for you. And even if you're happy in your current position, these sections may suggest ways you can add new dimensions and responsibilities to your job description.

No matter who you are, no matter what you're doing, you can apply each chapter in this book to make positive changes in your life. This book will show how you, too, can take that which has meaning for you, find out what you want to do for a living—if you haven't yet done so— or discover meaning in what you're already doing and make it more profitable for yourself.

In fact, this book will show that to be truly successful in the world— as a person, a company, or even a product—your actions must be rooted in integrity. You must develop an awareness not just of your own integrity, but of the integrity of your company, its customers, the marketplace, and your community.

Intuition enables you to accomplish those goals, and in so doing increase your wealth and profitability.

How This Book Can Help You

Each chapter of this book is targeted to enrich your professional life in ways you can put to use immediately. Practical intuition helps you rediscover and develop your natural intuitive abilities and then apply them in practical and profitable ways. No matter what your field or level of experience, you'll learn how intuition can help you answer all of the most important questions you face, including the following:

- **Career questions:** What career path will best suit my talents? What profitable skills or opportunities are available to me right now?
- **Investment questions:** Is the recent market sell-off merely a bull market correction, or the start of a bear market?
- **Hiring questions:** Which of these candidates should we choose?
- **Negotiating questions:** Should I take a hard line or make a concession?
- **Strategic questions:** Should my company form an alliance with one of our competitors?

If you read this book with the same spirit in which I wrote it, by the time you've finished all the exercises, you will be using your intuition as an integral part of your professional life. You will also be developing your intuition as something you do consciously and unconsciously every day, like exercise or meditation. And you will become aware for the first time of many previously unconscious thinking and behavior patterns and learn to use them productively.

Finally, you'll have a business plan for your career and your life. You will know where to go and how to get there. And you'll have fun in the process.

Practical Intuition™
FOR SUCCESS

—1—

How to Get the Most from This Book

How This Book Is Organized

This book has two distinct aims. First, it introduces you to a new way of looking at the business world. It also introduces you to a new way of looking at—and using—intuition. The challenge has been to present the material simultaneously since your understanding of the business concepts depends on your understanding of the intuitive ones, and at the same time, your understanding of the intuitive concepts will depend on your following the business ones.

The situation is not unlike that of the athlete who develops his strength through weight-training sessions in between sport-specific ones. A closer analogy might be learning a new subject in a new foreign language. Sometimes you have to pause for grammar or vocabulary lessons before learning the actual material.

As a result, we'll be moving simultaneously along two parallel tracks: developing your intuitive skills while creating and refining your own wealth plan. In the process, I will go back and forth between training your intuitive abilities and applying them practically to specific business situations. Like everything in this book, you should adapt it to your particular learning style and specific interests.

You can also dip into the book at random points as your spirit moves you. You may even want to try all the exercises in the book first—before reading any of the background text!

THE ONLY WAY TO DEVELOP YOUR INTUITION IS TO PRACTICE

This is a practical book to teach you a set of skills and a new way of experiencing and relating to your world. Throughout this book you will be asked to do a variety of exercises. The point of all the exercises is to change your perspective and give your intuition a chance to tell you things you might not otherwise have recognized.

The exercises in my first book, *Practical Intuition*, were designed to help you answer three specific life questions of your own choosing. The exercises here are designed to help you and your company become in tune with your market so that you are insightful enough, and adaptable enough, to profit in any environment. Even if you've completed the intuitive exercises in my first book, I recommend that you not skip over the ones here.

SOME EXERCISES MAY EVEN SEEM SILLY

The point of all the exercises is to change your perspective and give your intuition a chance to break out of traditional perspectives and view situations and the information they contain in new ways.

- Some exercises will help you develop your intuitive skills and habits; others provide regular, if not daily, "checks" to polish those skills once in place.
- Some exercises ask you to "become" the object of your attention (a product, a job, a competitor); others ask you to become a symbol of your "target."
- Some are designed to help you get in touch with your unconscious self; others will help you achieve detachment so you can view your situation objectively.

Even if you don't understand the point of a particular exercise, try to complete it conscientiously. I promise you that each one will help you improve your intuitive skills.

All the exercises in this book will give you information about your current career or business questions. You bought a business book because you are serious about your career. I'm sure you work hard and are busy, and I wouldn't dream of taking up your time with exercises that do not have a practical impact on your career success.

INTRODUCING BLIND EXERCISES

In school, our textbooks often provided the answers in "the back of the book." Here *you'll* provide the answers and find the questions later! Many of the exercises—including the very first one in the next chapter—will ask you to respond to questions "blindfolded": You won't know what you're being asked until *after* you've answered the question, and maybe not even then. For example, I might ask you to describe what the first person you speak to tomorrow will say. You won't know "whether you're right" until the next day.

These questions force you to rely on your intuition rather than your reasoning ability, though you may be tempted to "figure out" or "guess" the most likely answer. The point is to help you get in touch with your intuitive abilities, not to see how clever you are.

Some people find it awkward and even difficult doing exercises blindfolded. This response is natural. It's nothing more than the reasoning mind's frustration ("Give me some clues!") and its reluctance to relinquish control even momentarily.

If that happens, simply note your reactions and follow the instructions as best you can. Don't peek at the questions until you've completed the exercise! In a short while you'll overcome your resistance as you gain confidence with the feedback—and the surprising accuracy you'll discover. Eventually, even the most diehard skeptic will be won over.

KEEP A JOURNAL

It's important to record your responses to the exercises. Not only will this allow you to measure your progress, but it will also allow you to return to previous "readings" for review. You'll be amazed at how often an offhand statement proves remarkable relevant, if not prophetic.

What's more, history's most creative and productive individuals, from da Vinci to Edison, all kept journals to record their observations, and even minor thoughts. Journals are undeniably an excellent way for you to gain access to your intuitive and creative powers.

So use a journal devoted to your intuitive journey. Since many exercises ask you to give your immediate intuitive impressions without reflection or analysis, I strongly recommend that you use a tape recorder and transcribe your work. Unless you have superb shorthand skills, it will be almost impossible for your writing to keep up with the flow of your intuitive impressions. If a tape recorder isn't handy, jot down your responses to the exercises by using abbreviated notes and translate them later.

PERSONALIZE THE TECHNIQUES AND EXERCISES

This is a book about helping you in your business and professional career. In each chapter I'll show you how to apply your intuition to specific business situations of the sort you're likely to encounter.

If you're thinking about starting a business, I'll show you how your intuition can help you accomplish that. Or if you don't have a satisfying job and are looking for one, I'll show you how your intuition can help you do that. And if you already have one, I'll show you how your intuition can help make it more satisfying.

Feel free to modify either the chapters or the exercises to meet your own particular situation. If you're working in finance, you'll of course want to adapt them to your field. Someone in the medical profession would adapt them differently, although the basic process would be the same.

You may find that your intuitive process does not follow a particular exercise as I have structured it, but rather jumps from one step to the next, perhaps modifying the entire exercise. Allow this to happen. It is your own intuitive style revealing itself that will ultimately be the best path for you to follow.

Use your imagination. If a particular section is about starting a business and you're perfectly happy in your current job, perhaps you'll get some ideas on ways to reshape your responsibilities more to your liking. Or perhaps the new perspectives this book will open for you will make you rethink your current situation.

Even if you're a housewife whose job and career are making a home, you'll find ways to adapt these chapters to your situation. For example, you may not have realized that you are the employer of a team of part-time employees. Your "virtual" personnel might consist of your housekeeper, your painter, your grocer, your accountant, and so on.

WHAT'S COMING UP

Again, this is a practical book, so the best way to experience your intuition is to use it. As I do in all my live workshops, I'm going to throw you into the deep end of the pool by starting with an intuitive exercise.
   Ready?

~2~

THE INTUITIVE PROCESS
IN A NUTSHELL

YOU ALREADY USE YOUR INTUITION ALL THE TIME—THE TRICK IS GAINING CONSCIOUS CONTROL

Your intuitive faculty operates all the time. Every moment—right now—it is continually feeding information to your brain. Like your breathing, it takes place in the background. Your intuition operates without your having to think about it.

And whether or not you are aware of it, you have used your intuition in every decision—good or bad—you've ever made. When intuition operates unconsciously, though, the information it provides is not organized in any form. We have no idea how to apply it, so we randomly hit and miss with our "gut instinct."

The problem with the unconscious, of course, is just that: We're not conscious of it. So long as your intuition operates without your conscious direction, there is always the danger that it will move you in the direction of unconscious goals you'd rather avoid.

These unconscious goals are part of your "hidden agenda." Because your intuition does not distinguish between your conscious and unconscious goals, it will work as effectively to find you a *bad* investment—if your hidden agenda is to lose money—as it will to find you a good one.

In other words, you can just as easily use intuitive information for failure as for success. Since your goal is to become more successful, it's important that you learn to direct your intuition consciously. That's why you're reading this book!

WHAT INTUITION IS NOT

I wrote this book to show you how to use your intuition in your business and professional dealings. From that point of view, definitions aren't terribly helpful. Asking me to define or analyze intuition is like asking a comedian to dissect humor, or asking an artist to dissect beauty. I can do it, but I'm not sure the definition will help you use your intuition, any more than an English professor's definition of humor will make either of us stand-up comedians.

Still, it's important that you have some idea of what intuition is so that you and I are both talking about the same thing. There is a great deal of confusion and misunderstanding and New Age wishy-washiness about intuition, largely because the concept is used very loosely and is applied to a variety of cognitive processes.

Intuition is not creativity, though it shares many features with it. Of course, your intuition can assist your creative process in important ways. Your intuition can provide your creativity with more information to work on. Your intuition can also help you think "outside the box" by seeing past traditional boundaries and revealing otherwise hidden connections between things.

Nor is intuition "rapid thought" or "just guessing." Again, intuition is often confused with its characteristics. Because gaining access to your intuitive process initially requires suspending rational judgment—I emphasize the word *initially*—intuition is often dismissed as just "blurting out the first thing that comes into your mind" or "guessing." Just because intuitive impressions usually precede rational thought doesn't mean everything that precedes rational thought is intuition!

Similarly, intuitive impressions cannot be "explained" because they do not depend on logic or evidence. But that doesn't mean that every thought or feeling or impression you can't explain is intuition. Sometimes a gut feeling, after all, is nothing more than indigestion!

Finally, I would like to distinguish intuition from the "intuitive expertise" of a particular discipline. Every profession recognizes that an expert processes information and does things not just better than the nonexpert—but differently. True, experts often create the illusion of instantaneous thought by taking conscious shortcuts such as relying on estimates or rules of thumb to encapsulate broad swatches of their vast experience and knowledge. But over many years' experience, the expert develops "a sense" for his or her specialty that facilitates taking in a situation "at a glance."

An example of this is the salesclerk who knows instantly whether a customer just walking in intends to buy or is "just looking." Or the stock trader who "has a feel for the tape" and can tell when a stock is about to move. A similar case is the "aesthetic" sense of accomplished mathematicians and other scientists who can "just tell" whether a hypothesis is valid or not even before it is confirmed.

APPROACHING INTUITION FROM THE FLIP SIDE

We've been exploring what intuition isn't because that gives us a much better sense of what it is.

Branch Rickey, the legendary baseball wit and manager (Rickey was the man who signed Jackie Robinson) once defined luck as the "residue of design." Once you subtract all the hard work and planning that goes into success, what's left over is called luck.

We can approach intuition in the same way. When you take your mental processes and subtract your logic, your emotions, and your memory, what's left over is called intuition.

INTUITION DEFINED

What, exactly, is intuition? The dictionary defines it as "a quick and penetrating insight" or as "gaining direct knowledge about something without relying on reasoning." I see intuition as a process of gathering information without relying on your mental faculties and physical senses while at the same time being an extension of each.

You have five primary physical senses: touch, taste, smell, sight, and hearing. Your mental faculties include your imagination, your feelings, your memories, and your reasoning. Intuition gathers otherwise inaccessible information and makes it available through your physical senses and other perceiving modes such as thoughts and memories.

This additional information is then "thrown into the mix" along with your thoughts, memories, and physical sensations to construct your awareness of the world.

WHAT IF YOUR SENSES EXTENDED FARTHER THAN YOU THOUGHT?

Intuition can be an instinct for the pulse of something. Think of good investors. It's almost as if they can feel the heartbeat of the market and respond to it. If they can feel the heartbeat speeding up, and the quality of the beat shifting, then they know that three days from now they should be prepared for a boom, and they know that in the moment—right now—while there's time to act on their perceptions. If they get carried away with a certain beat and lose their detachment, they will also ultimately lose their investments.

There's nothing magical about it. We all sense the rhythm of our environment in a way that's far more profound than we realize: We call that gut instinct. The only difference between intuition and what we think of as our empirical process is that with intuition, our initial input is self-generated or self-perceived; it is not derived from outside sources. We "know" and then we look outside ourselves to focus, interpret, and verify.

Now, because we often see ourselves as separate from our environment, we use our senses to reach out for information. We use our eyes, ears, nose, mouth, and touch to tell us about our environment.

Intuition extends the range of what we think of as our senses. The following exercise is designed to help connect you on a visceral level to an extended range of your senses on a regular basis.

━━━━━

DAILY PRACTICE
JUST IMAGINE

Right now you are probably sitting in a chair or lying in bed reading this book. I'd like to direct your attention first to your body, your internal environment. You have internal senses and nerves and hormonal systems that keep you somewhat informed about what's going on inside you.

Now, for most people, their "selves" end with their outer epidermal layer; their skin separates them from the "world out there."

Now imagine a slightly "concentric" bubble around you. This represents how far your sense of touch extends your "environment." Focus on your sense of touch and see how far it extends.

Now imagine a slightly larger concentric bubble, this one representing how far your sense of smell further extends your environment. You can smell things farther way than those you can touch, so it encloses the first bubble. Focus on your sense of smell and see how much farther it extends than your sense of touch.

Imagine a still larger bubble, this time much, much larger. This represents how far your sense of hearing extends your environment. Focus on your sense of hearing and see how far it extends beyond your sense of touch and smell. Depending on the state of your eardrums, this bubble might be as large as a mile or so in diameter.

Now imagine the last bubble, this one extending as far as the eye can see. These concentric bubbles represent your environment.

Go back through these layers one by one, returning to your internal environment. Feel your body.

Now, one final time, extend your senses layer by layer. When you get to the final layer—move beyond it. Imagine your senses extending way, way beyond your sense of sight, connecting you to knowledge and events far outside "you," and then bringing that information back to "you" through your senses.

This is how your intuition functions.

◆～～～～

SIMPLY POINT YOUR INTUITION IN THE RIGHT DIRECTION

You can learn to direct your intuition far more easily than you probably realize. In fact, it is ready to work extremely hard for you. All you have to do is give it a specific task.

How? By asking it a question: "How can I refinance my loan?" "Which job offer should I accept?"

That's really all you need to do (of course, you need to know the "right" questions to ask). Once your unconscious has completed its work, your intuition will notify you with whatever clues it can provide.

THE INTUITIVE PROCESS IN A NUTSHELL

The intuitive process is actually quite simple:

• Get centered.

- Focus on a specific question.
- Notice the first impressions you receive in response to the question.
- Interpret your impressions.
- Verify your conclusions.

We will need to elaborate on each of these steps in the coming chapters, of course, but now let's jump right in with your first intuitive exercise.

EXERCISE 1
AN APPLE A DAY

The purpose of this exercise is to allow you to observe how you experience intuition. It will also reveal a lot about how quickly you will "take to" the exercises in this book.

Again, I'm throwing you into the deep end here. Don't worry if this exercise makes sense or what "the purpose is." Just try to follow the directions with an open mind.

Let's start by breaking in your intuition journal and developing the habit of formally recording these exercises.

Get comfortable in your seat. To get centered you don't have to "clear your mind." Simply spend a few moments to notice what you are noticing:

- What information are your senses revealing?
- What thoughts and feelings and memories are going through your head?
- How do you feel?

Now put out your right or left hand. Imagine that you are holding an apple. Notice how big it is. What it smells like. How heavy it is. Its color.

Now put out your other hand and feel another apple. As you do so, please answer the following questions:

Which apple is larger: the first or the second?
How much larger?

What other details do you notice about this second apple?

Record all your impressions, even those that "don't make sense." If you're not getting anything, record that. If you visualized something else (another fruit, for example), record that.

Stop. Only after you've recorded your responses (don't forget the details) should you turn the page to find the question you've just answered intuitively. It's printed in a footnote.

DISCUSSION

Here's how to interpret your impressions:

- If your second apple was larger than your first, you answered "up." In other words, your intuitive response was that the Dow Jones average tomorrow would close higher than it did today.
- If your second apple was smaller than your first, you answered "down."
- If your apples were the same size, you answered "unchanged."

You'll find out whether you were right in tomorrow's paper.

What does the size of those apples have to do with the financial markets? There's nothing mystically significant about an apple. I simply chose a piece of fruit because it's easy to visualize and, more important, completely removed from your actual "target." If I had revealed that you were predicting the stock market, or indeed that you were even answering a question, your reasoning mind would have interfered in the process with doubts and speculations.

HOW DID YOU FEEL?

Again, the important thing is not so much whether you were "right" but how you *experienced* the exercise.

- Were you correct about the details? For example, did you predict the *magnitude* of the change? Did you get any sense of other factors, like the stock market's volatility?

- What "distractions" did you notice and record during the exercise? Looking back over your notes, do they provide any clues?
- Did any other details provide telling clues? For example, did the color of the apples change?

Most important, did you find any particular aspects difficult? Many students find the exercise difficult—yet still get surprisingly accurate results! In terms of difficulty and accuracy, there are four possibilities:

- You found the exercise easy and your reading was accurate. Great!
- You found the exercise easy, but your reading was not accurate. Practice this exercise over the next few days and see whether your accuracy improves.
- You found the exercise difficult, but your reading was accurate. Your resistance to intuitive exercises will almost surely decrease in the coming days.
- You found the exercise difficult and your reading was not accurate. Don't worry. New skills sometimes take some time in developing. Again, practice this exercise frequently. You'll see that it becomes easier and that your accuracy improves.

Another advantage of this exercise for beginners is that it involves little "interpretation" of intuitive impressions. Keep in mind that most business decisions are more complex than a simple yes/no question like "Will the Dow Jones average close higher tomorrow?" In later chapters you'll graduate to far more sophisticated readings.

In the meantime, practice this exercise on a daily basis. Simply note your responses and follow up the next day with your feedback. It is an excellent way to get in touch with and develop your intuitive skills.

Quick! What Would You Do?

You own one thousand shares of a stock that just lost three points in the last half hour. It's Friday and the trading day closes in ten minutes for the weekend. Should you sell your position today or wait until Monday

Exercise 1. Here's the question you were answering: Will the Dow Jones average close up or down in the next trading session?

morning to decide, knowing that the stock could open considerably lower or the trading could even halt?

You're in a negotiation standoff that's gone on for weeks. The other party makes you one last "take-it-or-leave-it" offer and gives you until noon to decide. Should you accept the offer, reject it, or attempt a counteroffer?

We are frequently in situations in which a comprehensive intuitive examination, much less an exhaustive logical analysis, is impractical if not impossible. We also find ourselves in far less critical situations in which all we need to do is make a minor yes or no decision (Should you buy a computer this week or wait for a sale next month?) without going through all the steps in an elaborate "reading."

At such times you'll need to use the quick-hit technique to make a snap judgment. Since it's a simplified version of a full reading and calls for less interpretation and intuitive reasoning, it's like giving a reading "with training wheels" before graduating on to the complete process.

THE QUICK-HIT TECHNIQUE STEP-BY-STEP

The object of this technique is to focus your intuitive awareness narrowly on one of your senses. Quick hits always entail the following four-step process.

STEP 1: Get centered.
STEP 2: Focus on your question.
STEP 3: Notice your first impressions.
STEP 4: Interpret them in light of your question.

With practice, the process will become automatic and your intuitive response will come quickly.

The major difference between the quick-hit and the apple exercise is the speed and depth of the response.

A QUICK-HIT EXAMPLE

Here's an example provided by a student to give you an idea of how a quick hit works. Most people choose sight or touch as the sense they can identify and interpret most easily. Notice that the question is followed by a focus on impressions from one sense.

QUESTION: How do I get my supervisor to see things my way?

IMPRESSIONS: I close my eyes for a quick body check and then open them. I see a very decorative lamp and I notice that it isn't turned on. I see a wastepaper basket and I notice that I'm outside it (a strange observation, I might add). I see the hearts on the pillow on my couch.

INTERPRETATION: I interpret that right now isn't the time to try to reason with him because too much is going on. The "light" isn't on. A lot of "stuff" is happening. He is going to get rid of some things, but I'm not one of them. The trust between us is the basis for communication.

DISCUSSION

Notice here that intuition has given this student the ideal answer—to sit tight and trust—even though that isn't what the student would necessarily like to do.

Good advice from any source, intuitive or otherwise, is often hard to follow. When your advice is internally derived from your intuition, you must balance it with external feedback. In this case, perhaps the student can think back to all the instances in which trust in his supervisor was justified. This blending of empirical data with intuitive responses is the best way to use your intuition.

YOU CAN USE ANY SENSE TO GET A QUICK HIT

Sight may not be the dominant sense through which you receive your intuitive impressions. You can use any sense to get a quick hit. Here are illustrations of our other senses.

QUESTION: Will my company's bid on the project be accepted?

IMPRESSIONS: The first thing I notice after my body check is an unpleasant heaviness in my chest and a feeling of anticipation at my forehead. A feeling in my back of relief rather than joy.

INTERPRETATION: I take these impressions to mean that our bid will be accepted but it won't do what I had hoped for my company.

QUESTION: What would be a successful product to launch?

IMPRESSIONS: The water from the radiator. The sounds of my own body. The hum of my tape recorder. Someone closing a purse or a case. A beeping, possibly a warning signal. My breath.

INTERPRETATION: A program that helps people identify how operations are running with a testing element that automatically alerts the system to potential overload.

QUESTION: Will our new product outsell our competitor's?

IMPRESSIONS: A dusty feeling in the back of my throat, with a little sweetness from the bread I just ate. I'm finding bits and pieces of this sweetness everywhere.

INTERPRETATION: Yes, the product will do well because it addresses an essential need (bread). It may be slow in starting (dustiness).

QUESTION: Should our company hire the new candidate for marketing director?

IMPRESSIONS: Smoky, stale, heavy, dead air. No circulation; no movement.

INTERPRETATION: I think the answer is obvious: No!

USING YOUR MEMORY TO GET QUICK HITS

You are not limited to using any one sense through which to receive your intuitive impressions. You can also get a quick hit by using your memory to deliver intuitive information.

The technique is the same, only now you see what is the first memory you notice in response to a question. Memories are useful in the intuitive process because they contain many different types of sensory data that we've already integrated to some extent. When your intuition uses a memory to give you information, the impressions will already be "predigested" and partially interpreted.

REMEMBER: YOU'LL STILL BE INTEGRATING THIS INTUITIVE INFORMATION

The purpose of the quick hit is to tap your intuitive process when you don't have the time for a more thorough search. Training yourself to use it frequently also helps you develop your intuitive responsiveness.

Getting a rapid "fix" on a situation with impressions that call for a minimum of interpretation forces you to bypass your reasoning mind. I am not suggesting, however, that you base any important decision on a quick hit if you have the time to weigh the issues in greater detail, either intuitively, logically, or emotionally.

Whenever possible you should examine a situation from as many perspectives as possible to give a balanced reading.

<hr>

INTUITION IN ACTION

Walking home from work one day, the art director of a New York advertising agency smelled hot dogs from a vendor on the corner. Recalling the feeling of being at Coney Island with his father, he could hear the music that was playing that day. It was the day they'd bought matching pocketknives. In his mind's eye, he could recall the splendor of the sunlight and feel how much joy it added to his memory of that summer.

The happiness of reliving this experience, however, was fleeting, since he had other things on his mind. His biggest client, a clothing manufacturer, was dissatisfied with the campaign his agency had worked on for so many months. He'd even canceled a date with his son to work on revisions that he had hoped would save this important account.

He sat down at his dining room table to produce an entirely new campaign. He began to doodle, drawing Coney Island and his son around the picture of the product line he had to sell.

Then it hit him: The line would have more appeal by using a family image from bygone days. A clothing line that was easy to care for and easy to live in, but also one that had the simple elegance of classic styles, that was versatile and timeless.

He began to create a campaign based on the family theme, bringing the generations together in a "look" that could be adapted to each age group;

an indispensable part of the family image. Ideas flowed freely as he created the storyboards, sneaking in images from his own youth.

As a personal bonus, the art director was now working with ideas that resonated so deeply within himself that the campaign was a pleasure to produce. More important, he was reminded of the importance of his own son and family.

DISCUSSION

Had the art director been trained in the conscious use of his intuition, he could have directed it by using the quick-hit technique. As it was, the art director discovered it unconsciously.

The heart of intuition lies in our five senses—sight, smell, touch, taste, and hearing—as well as in our thoughts and the memories and patterns generated by our senses. If we open up these processes to the intuitive process, we give our intuition a rich menu that it can use to generate solutions.

VARIATIONS ON THE QUICK-HIT TECHNIQUE

You can have fun with this technique. In the old Groucho Marx television show *You Bet Your Life*, volunteers received a cash prize if they mentioned a word—"zebra," or "cupcake," or whatever—that had been previously revealed to the rest of the audience.

We can adopt the same approach. Here's one possibility: Fix a question for your intuition and then plant a suggestion with your unconscious to notify you in the future with helpful information as soon as you encounter a prearranged "trigger." For example, you might consciously suggest to your intuition that the very first time you see the color purple today, the very next thought or memory or impression will be the intuitive clue to your daily question.

You can devise your own variation. Experiment. See what works for you and what doesn't. With practice, you'll see that if you notice these seemingly simple "hits" regularly, this habit will be a powerful tool in having your decision-making be more effective.

INTRODUCING DAILY PRACTICE EXERCISES

As I mentioned in chapter 1, many exercises in this book are useful to perform on a regular, if not daily, basis. Like a good stretching regimen every morning, these exercises will help you develop and fine-tune your intuition habits. These routines will also help you develop a deeper connection to your ever-changing environment.

The first daily exercise was on extending your sensory awareness. The second one follows.

~~~~~~

DAILY PRACTICE
MY MORNING CHECK-IN

Take a few minutes each day to allow your intuition to generate any information you need to know without asking specific questions. Simply direct your intuition to give you information that would be useful to know that day.

Record your impressions and interpretations in your journal and note the date. Review them periodically, since they may reveal more detail and direction as events unfold over time.

~~~~~~

⁓3⁓

WHAT IS MY BUSINESS WORLD?
(IT'S BIGGER THAN YOU THINK)

WHAT IS INTEGRITY?

The dictionary defines it as "the state of being unimpaired; soundness; the quality or condition of being whole or undivided; completeness."

There is another sense of the word, too, though I am not referring to moral integrity here. I am talking about the communication between you and your ideas and goals, your team, and the environment in which you must thrive.

Integrity is the ability of a system to function effectively as a whole even though it comprises diverse parts. You cannot be productive if any parts of you—your values, your beliefs, your actions—are working at cross-purposes. Nor can you be profitable if you are not meeting the needs of your market, or if the market does not perceive you as meeting its needs.

Does that mean that everything in your business world has to be perfect in order for you to function effectively? No. But it does mean that the various interrelationships need to have mechanisms to maintain contact and health. The good financial manager knows that money can be made in any market, but only if you have enough clear contact with the market to be able to respond to the changes, or even predict them. Intuition allows you to perceive your environment more clearly and broadly so that you are better equipped to respond to it.

A metaphor may help. I have a visual definition of integrity, because sight is my clearest intuitive sense. I see my spine. If I do anything that's out of alignment with my spine, with the beliefs that make life worth living, then I can't do it effectively.

When you are working from your integrity, you naturally take into consideration your environment and your special understanding of it, the needs of your team, your strengths and your weaknesses. You also take into consideration what is uniquely yours to give to your environment that is also in keeping with what the environment has to give to your integrity and, hence, your success.

Intuition takes into account the well-being of the whole: the different agendas of our personal goals, our company, the environment and the market, and even the environment in which our market exists. At the same time, intuition creates an effective response pattern because all these elements are changing all the time.

BECOMING WHOLE AGAIN BY RECONNECTING TO YOUR WORLD

This is a book about becoming whole again and using that wholeness to profit from your life. In short, it is a book about rediscovering your integrity. How do we recover our lost integrity? For starters, we need to reclaim our creative and intuitive selves.

I realize that in today's cynical times, integrity has a Pollyannaish ring to it that may seem out of place in a practical book designed to help you get ahead. Unfortunately, most people and most companies are out of touch with integrity. As a result, their internal parts are not working together or are often at cross-purposes.

Is it any wonder that we don't achieve success or personal fulfillment? In an effort to be "logical" and "practical," we cut ourselves off from our emotions and our intuition. We've also removed ourselves from our environment and our communities; in isolating ourselves, we deprive ourselves of the ideas that feed us.

If we don't know who we are or what our goals are, how can we expect to understand, much less function effectively in, our company or marketplace? The same is true of companies, especially the leading corporations, which have grown so large and "diversified" that the original vision has been diffused, if not lost altogether.

So far from being "impractical" or "beside the point" to business success, integrity is absolutely indispensable. Again, I stress that this is not a touchy-feely New Age book on intuition, but a practical guide to helping you achieve success in the marketplace. But it may take some getting used to the notion that the most efficient way for a person to get ahead in business may be to take a step back and rediscover what he or she really wants, or to reestablish a lost connection with one's family. The shortest distance between two points—you and success—is not the straight line you may have imagined.

To succeed in business, your goal should be to create integrity with, on the one hand, what you want to do and what you have to offer and, on the other, the needs of your team, your market, and your environment. In simple terms, you're trying to build a house all these parties will want to live in. And when you accomplish this, the results can be extraordinary.

A BUSINESS EMPIRE FOUNDED ON INTEGRITY AND A DREAM

Once there was a young man who wanted to be an artist more than anything in life. Yet everyone said he had no talent. "You can't paint billboards, much less pictures!" they said. "You don't have a future."

But this young man knew differently. He didn't have a studio, only a mice-infested garage, but he worked hard anyway. He used the mice as models, drawing them in all kinds of situations.

But everyone still said he had no talent, no future. Against their advice, he set out for Hollywood . . . where Mickey and Minnie Mouse helped Walt Disney become the most successful cartoonist in the world.

This is one of my favorite stories. Trust your intuition, it says. Work in harmony with your life and you will succeed. Life is not about striving to make money. Money becomes an organic part of your life when your goals and your work are bound together with seamless integrity.

Walt Disney took something he loved, and nurtured, protected, and developed it despite the doubts of his friends and business associates. He took what he loved and then found a way to encourage other people to love it, too. And in the process he created an enormously successful business and he created it with integrity.

I recently took my son to Disney World with a friend and her daughters. What impressed me most about the experience was that the integrity of Walt Disney's founding vision has been sustained despite growing into a global giant. And don't forget: They are selling a mouse!

Despite the huge size of the organization, every staff person I met was truly excited about his or her job. Disney provided a showcase for their talents, and provided an organizational structure that encouraged them to share the company's values. What's more, because the company's values were clear to the world, it attracted employees who shared those values. These core values allow them to anticipate and respond to the needs of its guests, who, mind you, were also attracted by the same corporate values. Disney is now at a perilous crossroads. As it continues to expand and create new markets, Disney must avoid the many temptations to compromise its integrity in search of easy—but inevitably short-term—profits.

DISCUSSION

Even if you're not planning to launch a multibillion-dollar business, this book will show you how you, too, can take that which has meaning for you, find what you want to do for a living if you have not yet done so, or discover meaning in what you are already doing and make it more profitable for you. In fact, this book will show that to be truly successful in the world—as a person, a company, or even a product—your actions must be rooted in integrity. You must develop an awareness of not just your own integrity but the integrity of your company, its customers, the marketplace, and your community.

Intuition enables you to do that.

WHY NOT YOU?

A man wandered for many years, searching for happiness. Much came into his possession, but no joy remained. He came to Jacob and stood weeping, complaining about how he had been cheated in life. Eventually, he turned his head toward Jacob and moaned, "Why me? Why me?" And Jacob answered, "Why not you? You've looked everywhere else."

This is a short tale that Noah benShea relates in *Jacob the Baker*. Noah is a poet, philosopher, scholar, and internationally bestselling author. As he puts it, "My heart knows what my mind only thinks it knows." He explains:

Just before my thirtieth birthday and after almost a decade of public speaking, I became concerned that my remarks had become programmed. I could feel my mind searching its bulging rolodex of "inspiration" and the scent was disingenuous to myself. Fearing that I was losing contact with my own center, I sought to quiet myself.

The higher purpose behind my work had always been to make the world a better place. It was the transplanted ethic of blue-collar parents that reminded me I had been blessed with a capacity which should serve a larger purpose than my own.

While all my "do good" intentions to that date had been intellectual or verbal, I thought if I really wanted to make the world a better place perhaps I might think of feeding people or housing people. Herein was real need.

Out of this mental re-centering and a midnight internal-interrogation came the idea of opening a bagel factory. Bagels were bread, bread was the stuff of life, and even the Talmud says: "Without flour there is not Torah."

That kernel became a company which grew into a specialized bread manfacturing company with North American distribution and several hundred employees. I sold the business to a public company several years later but not before the character of a baker, whose life mimicked my own, was suggested to me by a friend and became the protagonist in several bestselling books which I have subsequently written. Ironically, the intuitive "right" move to the bakery brought both its own rewards and a return to center.

My experience on this journey has always reminded me of the wonderful story of a man who wakes up on the Sabbath and sees a pot of gold under his bed. Reaching for the money, it mysteriously moves away from him. When the man gives up, turns to his soul, and heads off to prayer, magically the money follows him. As the Yaqui shaman Don Juan reminds us: "Follow the path with a heart."

LOOK WITHIN YOURSELF

It is neither logical nor intuitive to look outward for a market and then make yourself or your product fit. Unfortunately, this is how we most often pursue our careers and live our lives. This may seem like a practical approach, but it is simply a "shortcut" that gets us nowhere—and often sets us back. It is intuitive to look within yourself or your company and find what it is about you the individual, you the company, even you the financial product that would be in demand from your market in a way in which your market or environment would give you what you need in order to grow.

There is an Italian expression, *"Piano, Piano, si va lontano,"* which means, "Slowly, slowly one goes far." Putting the time into conscious, directed action will ultimately save time and produce greater results.

You can possess that which within you is most precious—your integrity—and extend that outward to create success, instead of looking to create outside yourself that which you already have within. Everything that we seek to do well, and from our integrity, feeds our deeper selves. If you stick with your integrity, and what you love, you will always make your best career move.

Where Individuals and Companies Struggle or Fail

Success in business comes when your integrity is framed in a way that supports and creates a product that is naturally in harmony with the integrity or needs of your market—or is framed in such a way that it seems to be so—thereby allowing your market to nourish and sustain you as well as continue to accompany you toward success.

It bears repeating. You can be successful without considering your personal integrity as well as that of those working with you, your market, and your environment—but you will not be operating effectively and efficiently, and probably not for long.

Where individuals and businesses make their mistake is in not responding to the needs of these parties, or even themselves. Sometimes this is a failure in communication: Either they don't listen, say, to their markets, or there's so much "noise" within their company that they don't "hear" their markets. And sometimes it is arrogance or inertia: They don't know enough to listen to their market, or they get invested in and tied to what they're offering or how they're selling it.

Once communication breaks down in one area, it often breaks down in the others. Once a company loses sight of who it is and what it values, it is only a short while before the company will lose sight of its market. Integrity also involves the situation's meeting your primary needs. When you attempt something not in line with your integrity, you can't do it well, if you can do it at all. If you find yourself in a job or other business situation that does not meet your core needs, you have two paths you can take. The first is to see if you can find meaning by trying to find a way to describe your job to yourself in a way that has value to you. The second is to find a new path. We will explore both options.

Similarly, when a company attempts something not in line with its integrity, the company is offering the market something the market (or its team) no longer wants. Here the company must either reconnect with its market to find out what it wants, package its products differently in a way that its market will accept, or offer its market something else.

Apple Computer Corporation, for example, has been trying to sell its easy-to-use technology to the market in the same way for years, while seeing its market share erode dangerously. Perhaps its customers are now demanding something more complex and Apple's executives refuse or are unable to listen.

DEFINING YOUR BUSINESS WORLD IS YOUR MOST IMPORTANT STEP

Individuals and companies often take too narrow a view of their situation. "I'm looking for a job" or "We're offering a new service." If you are to succeed in business, you must expand your horizons.

To maintain integrity at all points within your business world—and without integrity your efforts will be ineffective or even counterproductive—you must constantly be aware of the parts as well as the whole. Generally speaking, your business world consists of four entities: you, your team, your market, and the environment. Keep in mind that we are using these terms loosely, and that these are not separate, static categories.

WHO ARE YOU?

You are the person (or company) offering a product or service to the market. If you are an individual, you are the "you." "You" can also refer to a company or other business entity. If you own or run a business, then, you can wear two hats as "you" the individual and "you" the company.

These shifting points of view may take some getting used to, but they will soon seem quite natural. The situation is no different from a person starting a business when they can be at once the owner of the business, the president, and the employee.

WHO IS YOUR TEAM?

Your team consists of those individuals or companies that help you get your product or service to your market.

If you're an employee, your team consists of all those people who help you do your job. Notice that this is not strictly limited to your coworkers. It might also include the receptionist of one of your company's suppliers.

If you're looking for a job or thinking of starting a business, your team still consists of all those people who help you do your job. That might include the all-night copy center's midnight shift who help you prepare your new letterhead.

And if you're a company, your team includes not only your suppliers, your employees, and your shareholders, but any other individuals or organizations that help you get your product or service to your market.

WHO IS YOUR MARKET?

Your market consists of all those individuals or companies who want what you have to offer.

If you're looking for work, your market consists of companies who want the skills and experience you offer.

If you're already working for a company, your market consists of not only your present employer but any other company that values what you offer.

And if you're a company, your market consists of those who value what you offer: your potential as well as current customers.

WHAT MAKES UP YOUR ENVIRONMENT?

Your environment is anything affecting either you or your market, so I don't mean here our green, ecological surroundings. Your environment includes everything from tax regulations, to the general economy, to social and political trends.

While you and your company are within your sphere of influence, you have relatively little impact on your market (although your product might) and virtually none on your environment. Your environment, your market, and your team, however, all have a great deal of impact on you.

YOU CAN DEFINE YOUR BUSINESS WORLD IN MANY WAYS

Again, it simply depends on what point of view you are adopting and whose needs and values you are considering. If I work for a company, I have my own needs, such as career advancement and personal fulfillment, not to mention earning a salary. The "market" for my skills and services includes not just this company but any other company that values them.

But to further my own needs, I must consider the needs of my company. The company needs to sell a product or service that meets the needs of its market so it, in turn, can meet the needs of those it depends on, including shareholders, suppliers, business or industry regulations—as well as its employees (including me).

GETTING TO KNOW YOUR BUSINESS WORLD'S NEEDS AND VALUES

If you own a company, for example, you need to know yourself, your company, your products and services, your employees, your shareholders, your banker, your suppliers, and so on. You also need to be in touch with the environment at large and how it affects you.

Conversely, if you are an employee, your issue is how to advance in the company. Your business world is made up of your personal needs and goals, as well as your company and its ability to notice your gifts and meet your needs. Your environment is your company and the divisions within it to which you can market yourself *and* the opportunities for your talents that lie outside your company.

Even if you are unemployed or have never worked, you can use these questions as the groundwork for a working model of what you could do. Your business world is you, yourself; your company is your talents and contacts; and the environment is the potential market.

As you can see, there are many aspects of your business world to consider. The next exercise will begin to give you some focus.

EXERCISE 2
DEFINING YOUR BUSINESS WORLD: PART I

The business world you define here will help you determine the goals you want to achieve as well as the steps you need to take to achieve them. This is not an intuitive exercise, but you should still record your thoughts in your journal.

What are the important components of your business world? If it helps, you can approach this by the categories we have discussed above: you, your team, your market, and your environment. Take your time. It may take you several days to thoroughly explore and identify every corner of your business world.

This exercise is the first of three parts. Having defined the various components of your business world, your next step will be to get in touch with the individual needs and values that make it up. You'll be doing that in chapter 5.

YOU CAN ADOPT ANYONE'S POINT OF VIEW

The business world you define from your point of view will be different from the business world your employer would define, or that your competitor would define. It is useful to repeat the previous exercise from different points of view. Doing so will give you insight into the values, goals, and strategies of others.

AN INTUITIVE TALE
Kevin Huvane, Managing Director, Creative Artists Agency

From the time I was very young, my mother impressed on me that my intuition, my gut, was always to be trusted. She would engage us in a game, posing a question and asking us to concentrate and give our first impression of what the answer or result would be. She sharpened our senses, our instinctual abilities, our intuition.

Only rarely have I strayed from those early teachings. Intuition has always been a part of my business thinking. Two occasions in particular come to mind.

I had recently purchased a book that was well received by the critics but not a commercial success. Reading this book was for my pure personal enjoyment; finally, I could read something without a business agenda.

I really loved the book. Throughout it, however, the image of one of my clients kept popping into my head. His image was constant. I didn't think anything of it and shortly finished the book.

Two days later, this client called to tell me about this book: He knew it would be almost impossible to adapt it, but he wanted to help make it into a movie. It was the same book, of course, and we ultimately transformed it into a critical and commercial film success.

Another time I was involved in some complicated and time-consuming negotiations with a company. On paper the company looked solid enough, but a nagging sensation prevented me from closing the deal. That same sense alerted me to certain discrepancies during the negotiations that I might otherwise have overlooked.

I trust my intuition because in countless other situations it has pointed me in the direction of opportunities and steered me away from trouble.

~~~~~

—4—

BEGIN BY NOTICING
WHAT YOU NOTICE

INTUITION OPERATES ALL THE TIME—
SO WHY AREN'T WE MORE AWARE OF IT?

To put your intuition to work for you, your first step must be to notice it. You must actively "extend your antennae" to become aware of the "supertext" of your perceptions.

Right now, as you read these words, your intuition is hard at work, feeding your brain important information. But if this is so, you may well be wondering why you aren't more aware of it.

In the first place, intuitive messages are rarely as clear and grammatical as "Buy five hundred shares of General Motors at tomorrow's opening price." Intuition usually comes in subtle and often symbolic ways.

What's more, we've also been conditioned to filter out intuition subconsciously, along with everything else in our internal and external environment that "doesn't make sense." Since intuitive impressions frequently fly in the face of logic and evidence, our automatic tendency is to ignore them.

You also may not be aware of your intuition because you mistake it for something else. When you are using intuition unconsciously, what you think of as random or "distracting" thoughts are actually intuition much of the time. If you're at an important business meeting, for example, and the childhood image of your father's clunky old station wagon flashes through your head, don't dismiss it out of hand: This may be your intuition's way of telling you that your own car is about to break down or that the ideas at the meeting are outmoded!

This reminds me of a play in which the main character is delighted to discover that he has been "speaking prose all his life" without realizing it. As you master your intuitive process, you may discover, like this character, that you have been intuitive all your life without realizing it.

YOU NEED A BASELINE BEFORE YOU START REPORTING

Step back for a moment. Remember that you are now reporting the impressions you receive—and this is important—*in response to your question*. Since you will be receiving impressions before and as you read the question, part of your answer is how your perceptions *change*.

Let's say that before you read the question you are aware of the smells of your dinner cooking, a heaviness in your right leg, and a general feeling of irritation. Then you read the question and suddenly you notice the blue cup on your desk. The blue cup is the intuitive information in response to the question. But unless you've taken a snapshot of what you're noticing beforehand, you might mistake the smells of your dinner, the heaviness in your right leg, or your irritation as your intuition's response.

So before you begin any intuitive—or even logical—process, you need to be aware of "what's going on for you." If you've been having a tough day, for example, and you sit down to do an intuitive reading, all your impressions may be colored by your mood.

EXERCISE 3
BODY CHECK

A body check is nothing more than a snapshot inventory of what's going on in you and around you in this moment. I refer to it as a body check even though you'll be noticing all your impressions, not simply your internal ones.

Here's what you should notice:

- What are your five senses perceiving in this moment?
- How does your body feel?
- What is your overall mood?

- Which emotion is most prominent for you right now?
- What thoughts or memories float around in your mind?

That's all there is to this exercise. The entire process should take only a few seconds. In actual practice, you wouldn't need to record these things, but for the first time, you should record your impressions in your notebook or with your tape recorder.

ONE PERSON'S EXAMPLE

I smell my aftershave. I see the morning paper in front of me. I'm feeling fuzzy, unfocused. I'm tasting mint. I hear the wind against the window. I'm wondering why I had an argument with a friend of mine. I wish I knew how to set things right or if I should. The phone just rang. My most prominent emotion right now is dreaminess. I'm remembering the letters that I was supposed to mail today and didn't. My overall tone is distracted.

DISCUSSION

Nothing surprises me more than the fact that people, by and large, are unaware of what is surrounding them and going on inside them at any given moment—what they smell, taste, see, hear, and feel; their thoughts and emotions; the memories and dreams that float through their minds.

Once you bring your preliminary sensations into your consciousness, they're less likely to play a part in either logical or intuitive decisions. Again, the idea is simply to notice what's going on for you in the moment. If you're feeling pessimistic, it's good to be aware of that because the simple awareness of a state will minimize its influence.

DAILY PRACTICE
BODY CHECK

As you know, body checks prepare you to receive intuitive information, and so are an integral part of the conscious use of your intuition. Since they take only a few seconds to perform, you can practice frequently at random moments throughout the day. You don't need to record your responses. Done regularly, this exercise will help you develop your intuitive awareness.

<center>~~~~~~</center>

DEVELOPING YOUR GENERAL AWARENESS

Intuition is a faculty that gathers and processes information for you. It's doing so right now, as you read these words.

To develop conscious control over your intuition, you must begin by developing your general awareness. I don't mean that you need to become more aware of your surroundings, although this will happen as you complete the exercises. I mean that you must be aware of what you notice and how you notice it. For example, consider the following questions:

- Which do you tend to notice the most: your thoughts, your memories, your feelings, or your physical senses? Which do you tend to notice the least?
- Which do you notice more: your internal world or your external environment?
- Do you tend to favor any particular physical sense over the others?
- In what ways or situations do these things change?

Perhaps you think that you're already quite aware of internal and external worlds. Unfortunately, in modern life we are all so bombarded with sensory perceptions that we condition ourselves to filter out huge chunks of our surroundings.

What's more, in addition to our external senses, our thoughts are layered with internal events. Each moment is dense with memories, thoughts, fears, hopes, and countless other feelings and emotions. These internal preoccupations further tax our conscious awareness of our environment.

QUICK—RIGHT NOW—WHAT ARE YOU THINKING?

The best frame of mind is to be conscious, yet we very rarely are. How often are you consciously aware in the moment—right now—of what is going through your mind, what you're feeling, sensing, experiencing?

Even as we are most aware of our environment, we're often not able to pinpoint what we're thinking about. If I were to ask you what you've been thinking about the last few moments, you would probably have to pause before responding—even though my question itself concerned the very process that you must engage in to answer the question!

The following exercise will help you develop your general awareness, which is an important first step in developing your intuitive awareness.

EXERCISE 4
REPORTING YOUR IMPRESSIONS

This exercise is both simple and difficult. It is simple because all you need to do is report what you are aware of in both your internal and external environments. It is difficult because you have been conditioned to edit out "what's obvious" and "noise" or "distractions." Your impressions do not need "to make sense," but it is important to include everything you notice.

Do not direct your awareness in any way. Allow this process to happen without relying on a "checklist" of your various senses, followed by your memories, followed by your thoughts, followed by your feelings. You'll notice what you notice.

And if you don't notice anything—notice that!

ONE PERSON'S EXAMPLE

The radio is playing "oldies but goodies." I smell my coffee. My face itches a bit; I haven't shaved for a few days. My fingernails need trimming. I could use a haircut. I miss my father. I ate too much for dinner. I feel this pen and the way it scratches the paper as I write. My body position in this chair is uncomfortable, but it almost seems too difficult to shift. My mouth's a little dry. Some coffee, iced coffee, would be nice.

DISCUSSION

There's no right or wrong way to do this exercise, so long as you report everything you notice without "editing" your impressions in any way. This exercise takes only a few moments to perform and can be done randomly throughout the day. Practice it often since it is the cornerstone of everything else that follows.

~~~~~~

DAILY PRACTICE
BEING "IN THE MOMENT"

Every so often, take a few moments to become consciously aware of everything you notice. You can do this anytime, on the way home from work or while waiting for your breakfast coffee. You don't always need to take detailed notes in your journal, though it's not a bad idea to do so whenever you are able to. Again: The key point is to report what you observe—to yourself or in your journal—continuously, without interruption.

~~~~~~

NEXT WE CONSIDER THE "WHY"

Now that you are more in touch with what and how you notice, you're ready to graduate to a more interesting question: *Why* do you notice what you notice? You're about to discover a startling truth.

NOW, WHAT IF EVERYTHING YOU NOTICED HAD MEANING?

Think about it. Every moment your senses are being bombarded by information around you: sights, smells, sounds, tastes, and physical sensations, not to mention the intuitive information we're picking up. What's more, your own mental environment is constantly stirring the pot by throwing in thoughts and feelings and memories.

Mercifully, we are conscious of only the smallest fraction of this welter. Otherwise we would be overwhelmed by the sheer weight of confusing information and find ourselves unable to function.

Somehow our brains are able to make sense of this jumble. Our brains filter out most of the information they receive and make us aware of selected information only. Now, here's a question I'd like you to ponder: How do our brains decide what information to make us consciously aware of and what to withhold?

We notice what has meaning to us. Things in themselves don't "mean" anything. A pebble on the sidewalk doesn't mean anything to me, but if my son picks it up and gives it to me "as a present," I cherish that stone.

And for our purposes, we'll define "meaning" as the way in which what we notice helps answer our questions.

IF YOU MUST—PRETEND

It bears repeating. Everything you notice has meaning. If you suddenly remember a song from childhood, that fact has meaning. Even if your nose begins to itch, your noticing that has significance. The trick, again, is knowing what question that itch is answering.

For most people this is a novel concept that they find difficult to accept. "You mean *everything* I notice has meaning?" they challenge. "Even when my nose itches?"

Yes, even that has meaning. Even if you have trouble accepting this concept, you can *act* as if everything has meaning. If I'm right, you open your intuition and expand your sources of information, and if I'm wrong, you will at least become more aware of your surroundings. If you don't believe in intuition, you can at least accept the possibility that you unconsciously know more than you think.

~~~~~~

DAILY PRACTICE
WHAT QUESTIONS ARE YOU ANSWERING?

In the previous Daily Practice (Being "In the Moment"), the aim is to notice what is going on in your internal and external environments. Now you know that all these impressions mean something. Everything you notice, in other words, is information that is useful in answering a question. The point of this Daily Practice is to search for the questions you're answering.

Start making it a habit to note all the things that you're thinking about *right now*, at this moment. Then note the things you've been thinking about continually in the last few hours, few days, few months. What patterns emerge?

Your intuition is always giving you information to help you answer your questions. What questions are you asking?

What questions *should* you be asking?

~~~~~~

⁓5⁓

WHAT DOES THIS PERSON—OR COMPANY, OR MARKET—WANT?

(CAREFUL: THEY MIGHT NOT EVEN KNOW)

SUPPLY AND DEMAND: THE UNIVERSAL BUSINESS FORMULA

Whether you are an individual looking for a job or a multinational corporation looking to develop and launch a new product, the secret to business success comes down to figuring out what the other guy wants, then finding a way to match that with what you want and what you have to offer.

If you're looking for a job, you must find out what companies in your field are looking for and then match that with what you have to offer.

If you're a company, you must find out what your market wants—values—and then match that with what you have to offer.

Notice that this formula governs every aspect of a company's operation. In addition to what its customers want, a company must find out the following:

- what its investors want
- what its suppliers want
- what its employees want

And in each case, the company must find a way to satisfy those needs if it wants its own needs to be met.

~~~~~

INTUITION IN ACTION

Edward C. "Ned" Johnson III relied on a "gut feeling" that he could attract new investors to Fidelity if a money market fund offered check-writing privileges. Despite this attractive feature, however, he couldn't sell the fund through brokers because an exhorbitant commission would have wiped out any interest rate advantages.

So he intuited another solution—advertising in newspapers and selling directly to consumers over the phone. These two innovations alone have completely reshaped the mutual fund business.

~~~~~

GETTING IN TOUCH WITH YOUR MARKET AND ITS VALUES

It would seem to be a simple matter to determine what your market wants. Just ask people, right? Wrong. The problem with polls and "market research" is that they are passive and reactive rather than proactive. A company would not survive for long if it had to wait for the market to give it direction.

An even bigger problem with asking people what they want is that they don't know. (On the other hand, people invariably know what they *don't* want—something to keep in mind if you ever poll your market.)

Let's say you had asked people in 1880 whether they needed a motorized vehicle. The car might not have been developed for decades. Or consider copy machines. When Xerox began, it was flying in the face of a market research study that estimated total worldwide demand for this product at $50 million annually (missing the mark by a factor of only one thousand). More recently, if Sony had asked people whether they wanted portable stereos in 1980, the Walkman might never have been created.

Finding out what a market wants, then, is not a matter of conducting market research or focus groups. Nor is logic and analysis going to give you much insight about the needs and goals of others. Let's not forget that we are only human, and many of our needs and values are unconscious and often "irrational."

Your market is not always in touch with what it wants—but you'd better be. In short, you have to get in touch with what your market needs or what it perceives its needs to be. And it is here that your intuition can provide invaluable insights.

I-MODE: TAKING THE PULSE OF ANYONE OR ANYTHING

Intuition allows you to embody a market (or a person, or anything else) and to anticipate its needs by addressing them as your own. Instead of analyzing a subject, which creates distance because of the distant perspective, you *become* what you're scrutinizing.

To know what another person is truly thinking or feeling, the old saying goes, we must walk in his shoes. I-mode goes much farther than that and says that these shoes *become* your shoes.

This is more than simply empathizing or identifying with someone or something else. You are using all of your senses as well as your memory, intellect, intuition, and emotions to "be" the other. In I-mode you should be able to know what the other person is thinking, feeling, and smelling. By becoming and embodying what you want to understand, you can sense their needs, thoughts, and emotions directly, firsthand.

It's the ability to embody a situation and then to use all your senses for information. And the funny thing is, once you embody it, your intellect will kick in, and you'll begin to notice in the real world facts that substantiate your intuitive impressions.

YOU CAN USE I-MODE TO BECOME ANYTHING

There is nothing hocus-pocus about this modeling technique, which has been used by some of history's greatest scientists to penetrate the mysteries of reality. Einstein "became" a beam of light to understand it, and in so doing created the theory of relativity. Dr. Jonas Salk "became" the polio virus as well as the body's immune system, and in so doing he developed the polio vaccine.

We are simply borrowing the technique and applying it to the business world, where it can be used just as effectively to understand anything. We've all used our imagination to "pretend" we were someone else, but with I-mode you can extend the possibilities to become any of the following:

- a person
- a market

- a job
- a company
- a stock
- an industry
- a product
- a situation

Once you "are" the market—or the product, or the industry, or the person—you not only know what it wants but know how to effectively communicate what you have to offer.

We call it I-mode because the letter *I* captures so many characteristics of this process. You (the first *I*) are using your intuition and imagination to identify with someone or something else. Which brings us to the important subject of integrity, another *i* word.

EXERCISE 5
DEFINING YOUR BUSINESS WORLD: PART II

This is the second part of an exercise we began in chapter 3 (page 29). Since most people work for a company, we will be considering their needs, their company's needs, and their environment's needs. You will be answering questions that define your business world, then, in three ways: as an individual, as your company, and as your environment. (You should, of course, be using the business world components you've already identified in part 1 of this exercise.)

First, do a body check to get centered. Now let's begin. Allow the responses to the questions to come to you instead of your searching for them. Record them even if they don't make sense.

If you are not working at the present time, the answers to the questions about "your company" may feel made up or contrived. That's okay. Allow yourself to feel this way but record the information that comes to you. If it helps, ask these questions from the point of view of a company you'd *like* to work for.

You may feel an answer to a question, or you may see it, or you may remember a moment in your past and allow it to be the answer. At times you may notice outside distractions, like a door slamming or a plane overhead. Record those, too. Suspend judgment and allow yourself to record whatever perceptions come to you.

Once you've recorded your interpretations, you can use your intellect to interpret and make sense of them. Our intellect comprises our interpretation of information gained through our five senses and our memory or experience, as well as our judgments gained from those experiences.

The "I's" below help you identify with each part of your business world and consider its needs and values as your own. Don't worry for now whether all these terms or questions make sense. We're at the beginning of a process, so you're just getting your feet wet.

"I" the Individual:

- What do you want?
- What do you need?
- What is your greatest talent?
- What is your most formidable obstacle?
- What part of your life are you the most satisfied with?
- What is missing in your life?
- How would you like your life to change in the coming year?
- What is your mission?

"I" the Company (allow yourself to become your company):

- What am I?
- What do I need to function well right now?
- What difficulties do I face right now?
- Where are my opportunities?
- What is getting in my way?
- Who are my best resources?
- What could I do differently to ensure success?
- What is my mission?

"I" the Environment (allow yourself to become your company's environment or market):

- What makes me say "yes"?
- What is missing?
- What do I want?
- What do I reject?

- What do I need?
- What bores me?
- How do I best accept information?

DEFINING YOUR BUSINESS WORLD: PART III

Now that you've allowed your intuition to provide you with information, let's allow your reasoning mind to consider the following questions:

- What do you want and need in your life right now?
- What are your talents?
- What are your weaknesses?
- How would you like your life to change in the coming year?
- What is your mission?
- What are your business opportunities?
- Where do you feel your opportunities are blocked?
- Who and what are your best business resources?
- What could you do differently to ensure career success?
- What is the goal of your career?
- What do you think you have that the market wants?
- What do you have that the market rejects?
- What makes your market say "yes" to products or ideas?
- What bores your market?

Now look at your original definition of your business world and incorporate it into your second definition of your business world, the one you did my way. Create a definition for each category that has agreement and integrity.

Once you've done that, combine the categories to create a business world for yourself that has integrity, a world in which you are doing what you want to do by using your resources effectively to generate something that your market wants. Record your description using the present tense even if these are projects that will take place in the future.

I don't expect you to find complete agreement between each category, or even to be fully in touch with what you want, much less with what your company or market wants.

ONE PERSON'S EXAMPLE

I am creating a company that uses my extensive travel experience and the contacts I have made on my travels. I will add a self-discovery element to the agenda by using the many courses I have taken over the years. It will allow other people to go to exotic places in such a way that they feel "at home" and safe while experiencing new concepts. A learning vacation with some spice would allow me to travel while still generating income. It would allow me to create wonderful experiences for my grown children and be paid for creating these experiences for others.

DISCUSSION

The intuitive process produces the intrinsic values of each "I." What's important to you? What works against you? Does that tell you whether one area is more important to you than the others? How easy or difficult was it for you to "become" each identity? Why?

Again, we will be exploring these questions in later chapters.

YOU SHOULD CONSIDER WHAT THE OTHER GUY WANTS AS AN AUTOMATIC REFLEX

I often see people and companies create brilliant ideas for products or services that they are unable to sell because they don't ask themselves the simple question "What do people want?" They forget that their market is an integral *part* of their business, not something they "sell to." Again, if you are an individual, remember that your market is your company. If you're selling something, your market is your customer.

The following two exercises will help you develop this habitual frame of mind when considering the needs of individuals first, and then of larger market groups.

〜〜〜〜〜

DAILY PRACTICE
LET'S PLAY ENTREPRENEUR

Even if you work for a company and have no intention of starting a business, you can still consider your company's market from an entrepreneurial point of view.

Let's say your company manufactures children's products. Your market is not children, but mothers and fathers and grandparents.

Now, use I-mode to become your target market and address its needs beyond those your company may already be satisfying. I want you to pretend you're starting a new company. Have fun with it.

When you are in I-mode, what does your target market need?

━━━━━━

DON'T FORGET YOUR ENVIRONMENT

Although you are not offering something to the environment, you must certainly take it into consideration when formulating your goals and actions. This is especially true today when every environment is subject to sudden and drastic changes that can devastate a good idea. It's probably too late now to enter the computer direct-mail business, for example; profit margins are too thin.

Again, the best way to stay in touch with your environment—and ensure that it is not working against you—is to use your intuition to "be" it, or in other words, to embody its values.

BEWARE OF UNCONSCIOUS NEEDS: HIDDEN AGENDAS

Hidden agendas are goals, needs, or values that we may or may not be aware of and that affect our ability to be clear with ourselves and others. We all have hidden agendas (the fancy phrase is "ulterior motive"). This isn't a cynical statement. Hidden agendas are not necessarily sneaky motives people are trying to hide from us. Sometimes, of course, they are trying to hide their real goal. A negotiation is a perfect example.

But quite often their hidden agenda is hidden even from them! In fact, the most important hidden agendas to uncover are the unconscious ones.

These unconscious goals are almost always in direct conflict with the ones we are conscious of. So it's vital to become aware of them if we are to understand ourselves, and our team, and our environment.

And just as you and I have conscious and unconscious goals, so do major corporations. Apple Computer Corporation, for example, has been shouting to the world, "Hey! We're simple. We're young. We're out there."

But it's not! Apple needs to be able to maintain what it perceives as valuable and essential in its identity, while being able to grow past the parts of that identity that are no longer valued by the market. By doing this, it will address the "corporate unconscious"—the basic values without which it could not function as a corporation—and the market's needs and its perceptions of Apple.

~~~~~~

DAILY PRACTICE
WHAT DOES THIS PERSON NEED RIGHT NOW?

Anytime you make contact today with another person, notice the first three perceptions you have.

Next, pick any two of the personal "I" questions you answered earlier and ask them about the other person. What does he or she need right now? What is his or her mission?

This is an especially important exercise to do with anyone new you meet. Turn him or her into a question—one of your personal "I" questions.

The same process works when you are dealing with anything new—a new group, a new company, a new industry, or even a new community. Use I-mode to become your target, and ask questions from its point of view.

~~~~~~

YOUR MARKET'S NEEDS WILL CHANGE

An accurate awareness of your business world—and your market, in particular—is a major influence in your course of action if you want it to be a success. Check in with it frequently by using the different techniques you are learning here. Keeping your finger on the pulse of all the components in your business world is important if you are to maintain the balance point of everyone's needs. We will explore this later.

~~~~~~~

AN INTUITIVE TALE

I've worked in the fragrance industry for twenty years and launched many very successful fragrances, such as Obsession and Eternity. I always knew I was intuitive because very often I would make strategic and creative decisions based on just "knowing" that often resulted in success.

The most significant intuitive decision I made was four years ago when I started my own business. I was working as the general manager for a joint venture with The Limited, having just launched and developed the Victoria's Secret bath business.

During a meeting with my boss, the president, I knew that it was time for me to leave my job to start my own business. I didn't have an exact picture of what the business would be, I just knew it was exactly the right time.

I called my best friend to tell him that I had made this decision. He thought I'd had a fight that day with my boss and my desire to start a business was just "reacting to something." He invited me to dinner to talk it over before "I did anything stupid."

I went to dinner with him that night and just talked. He saw that I had no anger or negative reaction to the meeting. By the end of the evening, he said that he really believed that I knew what I was doing and that he supported it.

I took the weekend to organize myself. The following Monday, I quit. No one understood exactly what I was doing. But, as in many times in the past, I just knew what to do.

Within six weeks, I had signed my first two clients, followed by four more the first year. After six months I hired a secretary and moved into a new office space. With the help of my team of nine employees, we have increased sales and profits in a competitive environment.

~~~~~~~

~~~6~~~

To Focus Your Intuition, Simply Ask a Question

You Better Know Precisely What You're Targeting

You must frame your questions precisely. One of the most difficult things in intuition is understanding what you're looking at. The job is made all the more complex when you're trying to simplify a question to a simple yes or no response.

Let's say you're considering the short-term purchase of a particular stock. Looking at the company intuitively, you sense growing sales in the coming months as well as an increase in the number of employees. Based on these impressions, you conclude that the stock price will increase.

You might be surprised, then, to see instead the stock price decline sharply. Your intuitive information about the company might have been completely accurate, but what you should have focused on was the *price* of the stock.

Or let's say all of Wall Street is waiting for next week's release by the government of the official employment statistics. The question you want to ask is not "Has unemployment decreased in the last quarter?" Instead, you should ask "How will the stock market react to next week's release of the national employment statistics?"

The same is true no matter what business decision you are considering. (I'll show you how to predict the stock market in chapter 22.)

WRITE YOUR QUESTION DOWN

Your mind is a messy place, and trying to keep track of your thoughts is like trying to find keys in a messy room. Writing down your question gives your intuition something more tangible to target, and forces you to be more conscious of what it is you're asking.

THE PARTICULAR QUESTIONS YOU NEED TO ASK WILL VARY

In applying your intuition, then, it's crucial to be clear and explicit about what you want to know. Your intuition is fairly reliable about alerting you to areas of concern, but it's still a good idea to approach your issues in a targeted and comprehensive fashion, taking into account the particular situation.

Real estate brokers, for instance, need to ask questions about three elements: their sellers, their buyers, and the properties. Here is a partial list of sample questions, first about the sellers:

- What is their minimum price?
- Are there any issues other than the potential buyers' offer that might induce the sellers to close?
- Why are they selling?

Here is a list of sample questions about the buyers:

- What features about the property or the neighborhood are most important to them?
- How high are they willing to go?

And, finally, here is the most important question to ask about the property:

- Is anything "wrong" with it?

Regarding this last question, you may have noticed in light of our previous discussion that while it's important to be specific, you should also phrase your question so that "close is good enough." There might be a huge problem—like a previous tax lien that no one knows about—or a tiny problem—like occasional water in the basement—that might gum up the works.

If you focused your intuition on any outstanding tax obligations, for example, you might very well overlook an intuitive warning to ask the seller about the basement. Sure enough, the broker discovers a leak before the buyer inspects the property. Fortunately, it's a small problem, though it would cause the buyer to scuttle the deal. So the broker has time to advise the seller to spend a few hundred dollars now to get the problem fixed.

IF YOU DON'T KNOW WHAT TO ASK, FOCUS ON YOUR OUTCOME

There will often be times when you don't know what to ask, such as when you are not familiar with the topic you're investigating. If that's the case, ask about your desired end result. In our real estate example, a novice broker might not know each specific question to consider, but he could ask his intuition, "What do I need to know to sell this house?"

Remember also in such situations to consult your intuition about whether you should desire the particular result: "*Should* I sell this house?"

YOU CAN ASK ANYTHING YOU WANT

The key distinction, as I mentioned, is that because intuition relies neither on your senses nor your reasoning, it can "tell" you things about people or situations that are outside your immediate environment and about which you "know nothing."

What's happening today on the corner of Broadway and Fifth Avenue in New York City already exists, even if you happen to live in Chicago. You don't have to assemble anything. It's there. All you have to do is find it and grab it.

AGAIN: IF YOU HAVE TROUBLE ACCEPTING THIS—PRETEND

Until you've experienced how powerfully effective your intuition can be in everyday business situations, you may find it difficult to accept the notion that your intuition can respond with accurate information about something—a person, a company, an event, or a situation—you "know nothing about." In fact, you'll see that the *less* information you have about something, the easier it is for your intuition to operate freely.

You don't have to take this ability on faith. In the coming chapters, you'll complete exercises that will allow you to prove it to yourself. Until you do, however, you can just pretend that your intuition's reach extends far beyond what you might consider possible.

YOUR IMPRESSIONS MAY NOT MAKE SENSE—FOR NOW

"Simply reporting" what you notice is not so simple now that you have a question in mind. In previous exercises, you simply reported whatever you noticed with no particular "direction." The question complicates the reporting process because you will now be expecting your impressions to "make sense."

Let's say that your question is "Will the stock market be a safe place to invest for the next six months?" And the first thing you notice is the sound of traffic outside your window; you may be tempted to ignore this impression—consciously if not unconsciously—as "just interference" or as "irrelevant."

But it's not irrelevant! The significance of traffic sounds may not be apparent now, but don't worry about that. You'll be interpreting and making sense of your impressions shortly. Now you're merely reporting what you notice, whether or not it makes sense.

"INTERFERENCE" IS A LOGICAL—NOT INTUITIVE—LABEL

Your intuition does not make judgments like "This is distracting" or "This makes no sense." So as soon as you become aware that something is "interfering" with or "distracting" your reading—a door slamming, someone coughing in the next room, the sound of fluorescent lights overhead, an irresistible itch on your right elbow—it's a tip-off that your reasoning mind is at work, jumping in with its two cents.

So in a sense, something *is* interfering with your intuition: the judgments of your reasoning mind.

WHAT'S MORE, "DISTRACTIONS" ARE ESPECIALLY SIGNIFICANT

Any impression that forces itself on you, that you can't help but notice, is a loud signal from your intuition. Your reasoning mind tends to "dismiss" whatever it considers to be a distraction—which is a fairly reliable sign that these are valid intuitive insights.

The Trick Is to Keep Speaking Continuously and Report Everything

As soon as you know your question, begin reporting immediately and don't stop until you're finished. You'll know your intuition has provided what it can to answer your question by a natural break in the flow.

Speaking continuously (or writing continuously, if you're not using a tape recorder), without missing a beat, allows your intuition to "do its thing" without your logical, analytical faculties getting involved.

Keeping your reasoning mind at bay is sometimes quite difficult, so I'll give you other techniques shortly. Again, you're only shutting out your reasoning process *for the moment*. Once you've completed reporting your impressions, you'll need your reasoning ability to make sense of your intuitive impressions and to see what logic "has to say" about your question.

If You Get Stuck, Make Something Up!

Why? Because you're not really making something up. What you're really doing is giving your intuition "permission" to retrieve information. Your mind always follows the path of least resistance, and it's much easier to gain access to your intuition and report what you notice than to exercise your creative or logical mind to "make something up."

Again, This May Not Be Easy to Accept, So Pretend

Once you present your intuition with a question, everything you think, remember, perceive, or in any other way sense is information to help you answer it. This may take some getting used to in the beginning. Remember that you're pretending everything is meaningful—that is, relevant to your question—to open up your perceptions. In a short while you'll be examining and verifying these perceptions with great care.

Now for a Real Stretch: What If You Didn't Actually Need to See the Question You Were Answering?

It's at this point that even diehard believers in intuition have their doubts raised. By now I trust you've begun to accept the idea that your intuition gives you information that is useful in answering any question you put to it. Now we're about to take the intuitive process to a more advanced level. I'm going to suggest that you use your senses, thoughts, and memories in a new way: to help answer a question without even knowing—at least not consciously knowing—what it is!

I realize that this may be the most radical proposition I've made so far. So again: Feel free to *pretend* that this is possible, at least for the next few exercises. At that point I'm sure you'll begin to see that you don't need to pretend.

INTRODUCING "BLIND" EXPERIMENTS

In keeping with our objective, scientific approach to testing our ideas about intuition, the next two exercises are "blind." When scientists want to investigate something, they frequently devise ways to prevent themselves from knowing what they are studying. The purpose of this is to ensure that they won't unconsciously influence the outcome of the experiment.

By doing blind readings, we ensure that we cannot influence—however subtly—either our intuitive impressions or our interpretations.

EXERCISE 6
THE ENVELOPE TECHNIQUE: PART I

You'll need to enlist a friend here. This shouldn't be a problem since this exercise is a lot of fun. Have your friend write the name of a person on a slip of paper, then place it in an envelope.

Don't try to guess or "figure out" the person's identity. Remember: Intuition is not guessing. This person should be someone your friend knows a lot about, but it doesn't have to be anyone you know. In fact, for this exercise, it would be more dramatic if you knew nothing about the person your friend selected. Your friend should know whoever it is so that you can get feedback on the accuracy of your reading.

You're ready to begin. Do a body check to get centered. When you're ready, take the envelope in your hand and allow your intuition to describe the person whose name is on the slip of paper. Yes,

I realize that you "don't know" who you're describing—but your intuition does. Simply report your impressions and interpretations, going into as much detail as you choose (the more the better).

While you are reporting your intuitive impressions, your friend should be recording your responses (if you don't have a tape recorder). Make sure your friend understands that he or she should not give you any feedback—either positive or negative—while you are speaking.

I say this because the other person invariably gives unconscious clues: a knowing smile, a subtle shaking of the head. You may find it helpful to have your back to the person until you've finished.

Only after you have completed your reading—both reporting and interpreting your impressions—should you open the envelope. At that point your friend can comment on the accuracy of your impressions (but keep in mind that you may have uncovered details about something your friend didn't know).

Most people who complete this exercise in my workshops are utterly astounded at the accuracy of their impressions. That's not to say that they're completely on the mark, of course, but the most common response is, "Oh, my God, how did I know that?"

As always, be sure to include your impressions and interpretation, along with the target's name and your friend's comments, in your journal.

THE ENVELOPE TECHNIQUE: PART II

Repeat this exercise next with a question (to which your friend knows the answer) and a company (again, which your friend knows well). If you have the time, you can try a variety of targets. It's a good idea also to try different time frames, the distant past as well as the present (the future is possible though you wouldn't get immediate feedback).

You can repeat this technique as a Daily Practice. The more feedback you get, the more conscious control you'll be able to take over this generally unconscious process.

> ## REMINDERS
>
> Don't ignore "distractions"! These are impressions your unconscious is forcing on you. They are distractions only because you haven't yet determined their relevance or meaning.
>
> And if you "aren't getting anything"—make something up!

One Person's Example

I feel a person who is heavy and can't move around very well. I see the initial K. This person reminds me of an uncle of mine who was the black sheep of the family and didn't amount to much. I feel someone who is concerned right now with covering a mistake they made a few months ago; I get February. The mistake was about leaving something messed up, like a hit-and-run accident. This doesn't feel like a very positive person. I don't think he's a good person to be around.

Her Interpretation

This stock isn't going anywhere. The name may begin with the letter *k* or it may be the initial of the product or president. Something happened to this stock in February that bears investigating. It doesn't seem like a good investment. Nothing is dynamic in the imagery, and there may be some danger areas that are yet to be uncovered.

Discussion

How did you do with your three envelopes? The feedback your friend provides will help you get further in touch with your intuitive process. Here are some questions you can discuss with your friend:

- In what ways were you on target?
- In what ways were you off base or even wildly off the mark? Why?
- How accurate were your interpretations compared with your initial impressions?
- How accurate were the impressions you "made up"?
- How relevant were the "distractions" you reported?

Keep in mind that even though these subjects were familiar to your friend, the relevance or accuracy of your impressions may not become apparent for months. You might report, for example, that the company is in financial trouble, but this might not become public knowledge until the next annual report. Or you might mention something about the person or question that your friend did not realize.

Now that you've had some practice doing a blind reading about subjects you are not attached to in any way, the next reading will address a question relevant to you.

EXERCISE 7
DOING A BLIND READING SOLO

On the next page a question is listed for this exercise. Don't look at it until you have completed the exercise. Instead, I want you to entertain the possibility that your intuition already knows the information that will be useful in answering the question.

Begin with a body check. Then take a deep breath and begin reporting your impressions. Know that your senses are already investigating the answer to the question. When you have finished, interpret what these impressions mean. Since you don't have a question to guide you, you'll have to trust that your unconscious knows what the question is.

Do this on your own before reading the example below, which might give you a clue to the nature of the question.

ONE PERSON'S EXAMPLE

I notice the freshness of the air from the window I just closed. I see a green bottle of mineral water with lots of clutter around it. I hear the ringing inside my ears and the workings of the machines in my house, the refrigerator. I taste a bitterness that I want to get rid of. I feel a pain in my neck.

I'm telling myself that everything will be okay. I'm thinking of how far I am from many of the people, places, and activities that are meaningful to me. I'm wondering if that is what life will be from now on or if this is just a passing moment.

My most prominent emotion is tension, mental tension (if that can be called an emotion), and a little anger. My body feels stiff from inactivity. I remember the sound of music and singing. I remember being young in a garden with dinner being prepared inside. I'm thinking of not wanting to go inside, that moment when playtime is over.

I feel guardedly hopeful.

INTERPRETATION

The perceptions are all about tension, clutter, and distraction. Actually there are some perceptions about the need to play, create, move, change things. A sense of being stuck and detached from what is important to my vitality.

When I look at the question, I understand exactly what my obstacle is. It actually confirms something that has been bothering me for a while. My work feels stagnant to me. I work in a family-owned business, but there isn't much family left in the business and my involvement feels like an irritation to me even though it's my livelihood.

I do value the company and the people who founded it. I've been reluctant to add my own personal creative vision to what is "tried and true" and still working. The fact that some of the employees were hired by my father when I was on his knee makes me feel that I have to adhere to a company program that has been imposed on me.

I have more to add to the company but I'm concerned about the resistance to change from the old guard, and I haven't been emotionally invested in the company enough to address the changes that need to be made.

DISCUSSION

Here's the question you were answering: "Who, what, or where are the obstacles to my career or financial success at this time?"

Only you, of course, can determine the accuracy of your reading. This may not be easy since some of the obstacles may be internal, that is, the hidden agenda we discussed earlier.

Also keep in mind that even your external obstacles may not be immediately apparent. A person or company you thought was an ally might in fact be a competitor—or become one.

REMINDER

Return to this and your other readings from time to time, since both the facts or your interpretations can change, and their relevance may not always be immediately obvious.

~7~

WHAT DO *I* WANT?
(YOU CAN—AND SHOULD—HAVE IT ALL)

WHAT THIS BOOK IS ALL ABOUT

The Italians have a colloquial saying, *"Campar' per lavorar' lavorar' per poter' campar',"* which means, "I live for work and I work to be able to live."

This is quite literally true for most of us. A good part of each day is devoted to work, so that if we are to live and not simply survive, it is important to enjoy and get "life" from what you do for a "living."

You have to understand why you're doing something. And you have to like doing it. It has to resonate with you, with your market, and with the people working with you.

This is as true and vital for companies as it is for individuals.

DON'T WAIT FOR A CRISIS OR A LUCKY BREAK

For most of us, career moves are not made until we lose our job, a better one crosses our path, or we become so dissatisfied that we quit. In doing so we forfeit a great many gentle moments of growth.

We should always be searching for a job—even if we have one. The successful businessperson is always redefining him- or herself from both internal and external points of view:

- How am I most marketable?
- Where and how can I make the biggest contribution?

- In what work environment will I be the happiest and most ful-filled?

YOU'RE SO UNCANNY IT'S ALMOST SCARY

That's what my friend on the other end of the telephone said to me. Someone had just bought out her company and she wasn't sure whether or not her job would be eliminated. It didn't matter to her that she hated what she was doing and that the head of the company didn't even know what she did. She had a six-year-old daughter, her husband had just started a new business, and she needed her job.

A few months earlier she had come to visit me one afternoon to discuss her work and career situation and get my feedback. I told her that I thought she wouldn't have to find another job until June or July, but that she might want to start thinking of what she wanted to do with her considerable talents.

As I was writing this chapter, she called and said, "You're scary; I just lost my job. My boss just quit for a silly reason, as you had predicted, and I have to stay on until July if I want to collect my severance."

I suggested—as I suggest to you now—that she take this opportunity to find a career she liked.

AN INTUITIVE TALE

Looking back now, I probably considered myself a person who believed in the reality of intuitive knowledge, and yet I believed that it wasn't reliable in any practical way. For that reason, I had taken it for granted that intuition was something that would never really be helpful to me. But this all changed about two years ago.

My place of business was undergoing the considerable institutional stress that often accompanies transitions in leadership and financial restructuring. A friend, who is a CEO of another organization, knew of Laura and her work, and he recommended that I consult with her, which I did. I was a little skeptical, at least at first, but willing to try something new. I met with her and said that I had some questions for her about my work. Without being given any more information, Laura proceeded to describe the overall situation at my organization. This was surprisingly accurate, and yet, in one sense, her description could have applied to almost any organization these days. However, she then described in great detail several occasions—meetings involving me and my colleagues. The information she gave was so detailed that it was as if she were actually seeing the events happening beforehand—as if she were present at them. This was incredible, and yet I would discover that the events did, in fact, happen just as she described them.

The amazingly helpful part of her intuitive descriptions of those events is not difficult to relate. It involves the detail itself; at least, it did for me. For instance, in one case, she said that if a specific person (whom she named) looks at you in a certain way, that will be your cue that this will be an extremely important meeting. Otherwise, it will seem to be a mundane, ordinary kind of event. Laura had given me a specific sign that would mean that the meeting would, in reality, have many hidden agendas and would result in some important decisions being made by my supervisor. Without the specific cue, I would not realize this was happening. She was exactly right. And she went on to give me solid, practical advice about how to present myself and who to engage and avoid during the meeting. She was exactly right about that, too. This was hugely important because, as a result, I received much more responsibility and financial security within the organization.

~~~~~

DISCOVERING WHO YOU ARE AND WHAT YOU WANT

Once you have become more aware of everything that goes on around you, you are that much closer to being able to use your intuition to determine what you want and the best ways in which to get it.

In the children's book *Are You My Mother?*, a bird hatches while his mother is away from the nest. He leaves to look for her, asking every animal he meets, "Are you my mother?" One answers, "No, I am not your mother, I am a dog." Another responds, "No, I am not your mother, I am a cat."

On and on the young bird goes. He finally finds his mother after figuring out what he is not. In doing so, he finds himself (and his worm-eating destiny).

You can target goals and set priorities in a similar way. You find out what you do want and what you don't. You discover what you should do and what you shouldn't. And you discover who you are and who you are not.

For many people, what they truly want to do is largely unconscious, and it is difficult, if not impossible, to approach the unconscious through direct, logical questioning (which at least reveals that we *don't* know what we want). Like that bird, then, let us begin to use our intuition by asking it questions. The following intuitive exercises are designed to help you get in touch with what you truly love to do.

EXERCISE 8
WHAT DO YOU WANT TO DO?

The following blind exercise reveals some quick insights into what you want to do by noting your intuitive impressions to several questions. As always, record your answers. Here are the questions:

- What are the first two stories or fairy tales that come to mind? What specific details of these are you aware of?
- What three activities would you do today if you could do anything you wanted?
- What are the first three words that come to mind?

ONE PERSON'S RESPONSE

Little Red Riding Hood and the Wizard of Oz. There was a movie about Little Red Riding Hood I was going to rent, and *The Wizard of Oz* because that's one of my favorites. It reminds me of the yellow brick road and Elton John's song "Goodbye Yellow Brick Road." It's kind of strange.

Ride my bike, maybe barbecue; play some basketball or other sport. Park, paint, wood finishing.

DISCUSSION

I tried this exercise on someone who had never done any intuitive training and was currently planning to make a living doing house-painting. He was having trouble starting up his business. I told him that he was going to answer some simple questions, and I did not say anything about intuition.

He thought his responses gave a clear sense that he should be directing his business to the outdoors, which was more in keeping with his integrity than painting interiors, as he had been doing. All of his imagery had either color or outdoor images in it, so painting was certainly a good job and a change, in that what he painted might make it a more profitable and enjoyable one.

The following exercise probes what you want to do in more detail.

EXERCISE 9
THE TOY STORE

Allow yourself, in your mind's eye, to become a child in a toy store. Allow the toy store to appear around you. Perceive this store and this child with all of your senses.

As you do so, consider the following questions:

- What kind of child are you?
- What are you looking for?
- Which toys attract you?
- Which ones do you examine but later reject?
- Which ones do you spend the most time with and why?
- Will you be able to take the toys home?
- Will there be more toys for you here tomorrow?
- What would you change to make this store more successful?
- What can you offer the store to make it thrive?
- Would the owner allow you to do this?
- What is the name of the store?
- What is your name?

DISCUSSION

The child in you is often the person who can suspend judgment to find the answer. Tap into that child or place of boundlessness, so that you can open up the boundaries to what you will allow yourself to do now.

Look at all of your information carefully. You may find literal details in your exercise record, such as the name of a company or person who has a job for you or the literal description of your next product or market. You will find that as you continue to make intuition part of your thinking, your imagery will become less metaphoric and richer in direct, precise details in "real life" language.

This exercise works if you either don't have a job right now or are stuck in one you don't like—because it gives you information about the kind of work you'd like to do.

This exercise also works when you're doing what you like because it helps you to do more of that.

━━━

DAILY PRACTICE
YOUR INTEREST SCRAPBOOK

On a daily basis, record what you are interested in, what you are doing in your spare time, your ideas or other peoples' ideas or actions that stimulate you. Clip articles that catch your eye, or pictures that move you.

After a few months, you will have an idea of where your interests lie. Create a large envelope to deposit all of these things into each day. At the end of the month lay it all out in front of you. Interpret this information in the same manner you would interpret any other intuitive information. Assemble it like the pieces of a puzzle and then look at what you have created. Try to see what patterns and directions emerge.

━━━

DISCUSSION

This exercise works by tapping into words and images and ideas that strike a chord in your unconscious. Again, this process is valuable even if you are in a job you love. By observing what your interests are, you will also discover which of your goals you may be trying unconsciously to sabotage. Becoming aware of this information allows you to make choices about what you value right now.

THE MOST IMPORTANT HIDDEN AGENDAS TO UNCOVER ARE YOUR OWN

You need to know the hidden agendas of others in order to function effectively within any group activity, whether it is a tense negotiation or a routine day at the office. But while it's easy and perhaps natural to be suspicious of another's motives, it rarely occurs to us to be suspicious of our own!

If you go into a meeting about recent changes in trade laws that affect your industry, for example, and your hidden agenda is to get some applause for the fact that you predicted these changes all along, your attention will be diverted. You will not participate in the meeting as fully as you could. More important, you would be vulnerable to someone else's hidden agenda.

Or maybe your hidden agenda is to get approval for the deal you've been working on for months even though it seems impractical in light of the new laws. Again, you leave yourself vulnerable.

Let's say you find yourself struggling in the marketplace despite your best plans and efforts. One likely explanation to explore is that you have a hidden agenda not to be successful. Perhaps it's because you feel you don't deserve success. Or perhaps it's because your unconscious senses that your business success may threaten your family life.

Hidden agendas often represent the conflicts between the various spheres in your business environment. Indeed, you may have uncovered some hidden agendas of your own when you answered the defining-the-business-world questions on pages 42–4.

Many women in difficult relationships get real estate licenses to become more independent. Consciously, that's their goal. But they fail to sell even a single home. Why? Because they're not ready to be independent. Unconsciously they want to stay dependent, so instead of their intuition working to help them, it's working against them.

You are not the master of your own mind; your unconscious is. But if you dedicate yourself to a course of action consciously, the chances are that you will succeed.

Once you are conscious of something—anything—you are more able to make the choice to move beyond it. And you *can* transcend your hidden agendas.

SOMETIMES YOU JUST NEED TO FRAME YOUR GOALS DIFFERENTLY

It's terribly important to understand your own integrity. To perform consistently at your best, you cannot afford to work against yourself and your goals.

At various times in my life, I've used intuition in ways that did not resonate with my integrity, but for survival reasons, I had to use it in that way. For example, just to make money for money's sake. I almost had to trick myself to be able to do it. For most people, I think you need to reframe what you want to do in order to make it work. We're whole, living organisms, yet we keep thinking we can use one part and neglect, suppress, or deny the rest.

If you're trying to succeed in sales but you're really shy, then you have to figure out a way to make that work for you. Yes, you're shy, but you're also sincere. Sincerity sells. Just make sure that what you're selling is compatible with your values so that you are not expending your energy working against yourself. Selling consulting services, for example, takes a long time because prospects want to get to know and respect you, a process that you, as a sincere person, can excel at. Selling Ginsu knives, on the other hand, just requires a ripe tomato!

You also need to find a way to frame goals for yourself so that you are not working at cross-purposes internally. My need to exercise, for example, interferes with my need to work. So I now do yoga rather than aerobics since I can frame yoga to increase my concentration—important in my work.

INTEGRITY REQUIRES BUSINESS *AND* PLEASURE

Conventional wisdom has it that business comes before pleasure. Not only does this approach *not* increase our efficiency, it actually *decreases* it by setting up a situation in which competing internal needs pull us in opposing directions. The whole point of integrity is to have all your engines—or as many engines as possible—pulling you in the same direction.

You really need to know if your conscious objectives and your unconscious motivations will be able to work together. You need to be aware of conflict so that your conscious commitment or awareness can keep your unconscious from pulling you in a direction you don't want to go.

Take a quick scan of your life. When did you make your best life moves, business or otherwise? How did you feel about life then? What were your objectives? Do a very short, snappy history of yourself.

You Might Want a Lot

You may discover that you want so many things, you don't even know where to begin.

It's important to prioritize your options. This can be in terms of what the market wants or in terms of your needs. Again, there's usually a creative solution that allows you to meet as many of your business world's needs as possible.

For Now, Just Decide What You Want

A good friend, Meagan, would often entertain embarking on the most outlandish projects about which we, her friends and I, would tease her incessantly. Once it was to get a role in a film; another time it was to meet the man of her dreams (in Los Angeles) and get married.

It wasn't that Meagan's expectations were so odd, but that she expected them to unfold exactly as she foresaw. I would tease, "There's Meagan, one hundred percent committed," making a play on words with "commitment" in the psychiatric sense.

Her optimistic expectations were met so often that she found it difficult to accept the rare disappointments. She took these moments as times of failure and would fall into a "I-can't-really-do-this" pit, the "who-am-I-kidding" doldrums. I felt that these were the moments when her unconscious would actually create barriers to her goal as important lessons that she needed to master. I have never seen Meagan get less than what she wanted.

Pretending is a powerful mental resource that allows us to experiment with "impossible" concepts.

EXPECT WHAT YOU WANT TO CHANGE

Don't feel that you must decide what you want to do "for the rest of your life." Our interests change over time. Our careers and our approach to those careers need to adapt if we are to continue to work at our fullest potential.

Much of today's job dissatisfaction comes from a refusal to acknowledge and adapt to changing situations. Many people are going out and trying to get the same job they just lost, when they could get a much better job by using their intuition.

8

INTERPRET WHAT YOU REPORT

GET YOUR IMPRESSIONS FIRST, THEN INTERPRET THEM

Receiving your intuitive impressions is like gathering together in one place many pieces of a puzzle. The next step is putting those pieces together to make sense of them—in other words, to see in what way they help answer your question.

Let's see how this works in practice. A consultant who is preoccupied with a pending deal jots down her impressions. Once she's recorded her impressions, she quickly interprets them. Here first are her impressions:

- an image of fruit trees
- the sound of birds singing
- the name "Paul"
- a feeling of caring
- a door in her house that doesn't close properly
- the underdone steak she was served for lunch

Here is how she interpreted her impressions:

- An image of fruit trees: The deal may be worthwhile in the long term even if it doesn't immediately "bear fruit."
- The sound of birds singing: The deal may come to fruition in the spring.

- The name "Paul": She might need to watch out for someone named Paul.
- A feeling of caring: She can try using a more personal approach in the negotiation.
- A door in her house that doesn't close properly: There might be trouble closing the deal.
- The underdone steak she was served for lunch: She'll need to be better prepared to conclude the deal.

Of course, our consultant may not choose to act on any of these impressions. Notice that some are incomplete. It isn't clear, for example, what role "Paul" will play in the negotiations, and whether he will be helpful or disruptive. Still, she is now on the lookout. Paying attention to these intuitive impressions will make her more aware of potential opportunities and pitfalls and allow her to proceed more confidently.

THE MEANING IS NOT ALWAYS APPARENT, SO REVIEW YOUR IMPRESSIONS FROM TIME TO TIME

Keep in mind that the meaning or relevance of a particular impression may not become obvious for a while. In our previous example regarding the consultant, "Paul" might not enter the picture for months, if indeed ever.

Moreover, as you develop over time and gain new experiences and perspectives, you'll discover nuances that had escaped you in your earlier interpretations, in much the same way that a second viewing of a movie always reveals aspects and elements you hadn't noticed previously. Every time you return to your impressions you will enjoy yet another "aha!" experience. This is another reason for my stressing the importance of your keeping an intuition journal.

WITH PRACTICE YOU WILL LEARN TO INTERPRET YOUR IMPRESSIONS AS YOU REPORT THEM

Again, until you develop some proficiency with your intuitive process, it's a good idea to keep the reporting and interpreting stages distinct. As you accustom yourself to using your intuition and get feedback with your readings, you'll become more efficient in the process.

Initially when people train in intuition, they get a lot of imagery and metaphor that need to be interpreted. They notice so many things that they're almost overwhelmed. With practice, the process begins to occur unconsciously. One day you'll find yourself translating your impressions *as* you report them, and your reading will effortlessly become as natural as a conversation.

∼9∼

WHAT DO I HAVE—AND WANT— TO OFFER?
(IT'S ALWAYS MORE THAN YOU THINK)

GETTING IN TOUCH WITH "YOU" AND WHAT YOU HAVE TO OFFER

An accurate determination of who "you" are and what you have to offer your market is the single most important factor in achieving success. To maintain your personal integrity, you must offer the market a skill you *want* to offer it.

You have many skills and abilities, but not all of them are ones you would want to find work doing. If you're a painter, you probably wouldn't want to direct traffic or hand out parking tickets, although I'm sure you would be quite capable of doing both.

Whether you are an individual or a company, however, your market must see value to them in what you have—and want—to offer.

TAKING STOCK OF YOUR SKILLS AND ASSETS

Once you know what you want to do, the next step is to see what you can offer the marketplace. You began this process by answering the first set of defining questions (see pages 42–4) and by updating your answers periodically.

In the next exercise I'd like you to be more specific.

EXERCISE 10
WHAT YOU BRING TO THE TABLE

The first part of this exercise is to list every single skill you can think of, every single strength. Even the things you do every day can be skills and strengths. (You make a wicked Halloween costume, a stunning origami airplane. You can say "hello" in twelve languages, "walk the dog" with your yo-yo, calculate on an abacus, mimic any animal sound.)

Really let loose here. Don't be afraid to be silly or trivial, and it's okay to brag. Take what you have and pretend it's all an asset, even if others don't think so and, especially, even if you don't think so.

One skill or strength may suggest others. For example, if you say "I am a good mother," explore the skills and strengths that this embodies: I am good at creating agreement between people. I am good at taking care of others. I am good at listening. I am good at making mundane things interesting, I am good at getting people to do what they are supposed to do.

The second part of this exercise is to take that list of skills and strengths and write a job description for yourself. You will be surprised by the number of diverse opportunities that will make themselves available.

The third part of this exercise is to figure out how you can make this job description salable and to what market.

DISCUSSION

Take your time on this exercise. Don't feel you have to complete it in one sitting. Also, it's sometimes hard seeing our own skills. We're too close to them.

A friend of mine once discovered that sitting around in her flannel nightgown and reading the newspaper was a skill. Here's her story.

~~~~~~

INTUITION IN ACTION

A few years ago, I left a fast-track executive communications job at a Fortune 500 corporation because I lost faith in the company. I also realized that playing politics would be my ticket to a promotion, and I wasn't very good at that.

Suddenly, for the first time, I discovered I had absolutely no purpose and no focus in my life. Even though I had left the company voluntarily, I hadn't really planned my next step, so I was stunned to discover that I "didn't know what I wanted to be when I grew up" and I was already thirty-four. I tried to intellectualize my way out of the situation, but I only ended up with "analysis paralysis." It got so bad that I'd spend my entire day in a flannel nightgown reading the paper and not hunting for a job at all.

Fortunately, I was so desperate I was willing to do anything to change things. I started with the obvious: "In a dysfunctional state like yours," I said to myself, "it's entirely legitimate to say that one of your chief goals is to take a shower and get dressed!" This caught me off guard and made me laugh. The rest was comparatively easy.

"If you had only one week to live," I asked myself, "and you could start and finish anything you wanted in that week, what would you do?"

"Write," I thought, without hesitation.

"Okay, what would you write?"

"A play. The Great American Play."

"Have you ever written a play before?"

"No."

"What makes you think you can?"

"I just know I can. I'm a good writer, and I can write in a lot of different styles and formats."

"What would you write about?"

"A story I just read in the paper today." (See, there was a good reason for reading the paper all day.)

"So what's stopping you?"

"I have to earn a living."

"So what could you do for money that would complement what you want to do for love so that you can bring the best of yourself to both jobs?"

"I could write corporate speeches, because writing speeches is a lot like writing dialogue."

That internal conversation lasted only a few minutes, but in that time, I discovered how I could become successful while beginning to do what I really wanted to do. My intuition gave me the answer, and then I used common sense to make it workable.

~~~~~

DISCUSSION

Today, that woman owns her own company and makes a solid six-figure income writing for corporations and prominent individuals. Because she has become one of the top corporate communication specialists in the country, she has worked with some of the most influential people in the world. These individuals can give her the entry she needs with top producers and directors to get her play produced in the best venue with the best actors.

In less than a minute, she used intuition to turn her professional life around. She could have applied the same approach to finding a satisfying job rather than starting a new business. That's what intuition does: It uses everything you have as material, right down to your flannel nightgown. It uses all your impressions, even the ones you're not paying close attention to, like what you're reading in the paper.

Everything in your life, every moment of the day, is grist for your intuition. Your job is to pay better attention to what your intuition is telling you.

DON'T WORRY ABOUT WHETHER YOU'RE "QUALIFIED"— WHERE YOUR INTERESTS LIE, YOUR ABILITY WILL DEVELOP

We are taught to think that education consists of a defined course of training. Some of our most successful individuals, however, are self-taught men and women with little formal education or training in their fields.

I call it "learning by osmosis." The state of openness and excitement with which people pursue their interests is the most intuitive and complete form of learning, and often you will not know what course of study you have chosen until it is nearing completion.

Intuition is the particular skill and language that is truest to my integrity. Everything that you are exposed to and everything that you are interpreting is part of learning, and each of these things can be used in a powerful way for you by shining it through your intuitive lens.

BE WILLING TO COMPROMISE

Before you try to find the precise fit between what you want to offer and what the marketplace is willing to pay for, you should approach what you want uncompromisingly. Of course, you may have to do a reality check. If you're fifty, you may not be able to become a successful professional ballerina. On the other hand, you probably could manage a thriving dance school or create an over-fifty dance company. (Can you imagine the publicity potential in that one?)

Over the short term, however, you may have to compromise on your "wish list" of dream jobs. I've worked with many actors over the years, some of whom have become major stars. The ones who met with far less success illustrate the most common mistake made in any kind of professional endeavor. They became caught up in what they wanted to offer the market ("I'm a serious actress, I won't do comedy") at the expense of recognizing what the market was looking for.

Today, for example, people want to be thin. There is a booming business in slimming products, books, clothing, exercise plans. If you're a developer of computer software, say, there is a software market within the weight loss field for you, too—if you want it. You could create a behaviorally based eating program using software that tailored its instructions to each individual through an interactive series of questions generated by the computer at the end of each day.

~10~

CREATE VERIFIABLE SCENARIOS

WHERE WE ARE SO FAR

You started with a body check to get yourself centered and ready to receive intuitive information. You then focused your intuition on a specific, targeted question and began reporting everything you noticed in response to that question. In the last intuition chapter, you began to interpret your impressions.

I told you not to "try" to notice anything, but rather simply to be aware of what you did notice—even "distractions." Now we're going to help direct the process a bit in a semisystematic way by shifting your attention to specific questions. I say "semisystematic" because you don't want to interfere with the natural flow of intuitive information.

INTRODUCING INTUITIVE REASONING

Using your intuition, as you know, involves a lot more than simply following a gut hunch. The problem is that people rarely follow up their hunch with further questions.

Let's say you get a hunch that your company's major competitor will release a great new product later this year that will cut into your market share in a big way. Clearly, this is a matter for some hard empirical investigation, but don't let your intuition off the hook yet—ask it for further details. What is this product like? Which of your customers will you most likely lose? Should you make your own preemptive announcement of a price reduction? What time of year will the product be released?

This is an illustration of intuitive reasoning. You ask a question and get impressions, which suggest new questions that lead to other impressions, and so on. It's rather like the process of a detective following a trail of clues. You simply "look to the side" of your initial impression to see what you notice. Of course, I mean "look" in the general sense rather than the strictly visual one.

YOUR GOAL IS TO CREATE COMPLETE, COHESIVE, VERIFIABLE SCENARIOS

It's important to hunt for more details for two reasons. First, as we just discussed, you'll have more information you can incorporate into your overall decision-making process. As a general rule, the longer we think about something the more muddled our ideas become as we generate more questions than our logical capacity can organize and handle.

With intuition, the opposite occurs. As you assemble your impressions, you keep adding pieces to the puzzle, and gradually a complete picture emerges.

How will you know when you have "enough" information? That depends, though generally there will be a natural break to your impressions. If, for example, your impressions seem to conflict, you have a strong clue to the fact that you need to ask more questions to make sense of the apparent contradiction.

You're wondering whether you should accept a lucrative job offer that would mean quitting your present job. You look at the offer intuitively and get a sense of a candle's beautiful flame attracting you, but then you sense it burning your hand. You need to ask your intuition further questions to resolve this mixed message. Perhaps the company making the job offer will let you go in a year. Perhaps it will go out of business. These are obviously questions worth investigating.

Perhaps even more important is that you can use these additional details to verify your intuitive hits in an objective, almost scientific way.

You're the fashion director of a major clothing company trying to get a sense of what will be "hot" next season. Your gut tells you that hem lines will be very long next year. How can you verify this impression? Well, one way would be to consult your intuition about shoe styles. What's this? Now your gut tells you that high boots will be all the rage. But high boots go with shorter skirt lengths, not longer ones. Obviously now you must "look to the side" for more details to see whether you can resolve this confusion or, if not, determine which of your impressions was accurate.

REMINDER

Your intuitive impressions are always accurate, although your interpretation of them can lead you astray.

INTRODUCING TIME LINES

As the name suggests, a time line is a verifiable scenario in chronological order. While a scenario typically consists of detailed impressions surrounding a particular object or event, a time line consists of a *sequence* of events leading up to the one you're considering.

It's important to "circle" any important event with others that serve as markers so that you can have a sense of what leads up to it, where you might want to intervene, and if, indeed, it will actually occur. While you can usually verify intuitive impressions about the present, by the time you've verified those about a future event, it's too late to act.

Time lines are your advance warning system. Since many if not most of your business decisions involve planning, time lines will be an invaluable tool in your intuitive and decision-making arsenal.

HERE'S HOW THEY WORK

You get an intuitive impression about an important event that takes place some time in the future, only you have to take steps before it happens—if not immediately. At the same time, to verify your impressions, you ask your intuition about other events leading up to the major one. These events don't have to be related in any way but they must precede it.

Let's say you get a sense that minor events A and B will precede major event C. You then generate more intuitive information about the two preceding occurrences. You may find as you do this that you'll discover other events to add to your time line as well as information as to why the outcome you're asking about is likely (or unlikely) to occur. If events A and B fail to unfold as you had anticipated, the chances are that neither will major event C.

AN ILLUSTRATION

Let's say that I get the sense that the price of a QuantumCom Corporation stock, a major holding in my portfolio, is going to decline sharply next month and I want to know whether I should sell my shares. The stock has been steadily increasing since it reported a new joint venture, but my intuition warns me that one of its patents is in trouble.

My problem is that if I wait for confirmation of patent trouble, the share prices may plummet before I have a chance to sell. I need to ask my intuition for events that will precede QuantumCom's patent problems, and get as many details surrounding those events as possible.

When I look at the situation intuitively, I get the sense that the Japanese yen will fall in value relative to the dollar a week or two before QuantumCom's imminent problems. I also get the sense that there will be flooding in Kansas a day or two before the share prices drop.

By creating this scenario, I have an early warning system that allows me to act in time. If the yen plunges and there are floods in the Midwest, the rest of the scenario is probably right and I can hold on to my shares of QuantumCom. If, on the other hand, the yen *rises* in value and the Midwest experiences a drought, then the rest of my reading was probably also off the mark. I now have time to sell my shares.

The events on your time line need not be related in any way to your outcome. They're simply "markers" to give you a sense of whether or not your interpretation is on the right track. Yen prices, flooding in the Midwest, and the takeover of QuantumCom Corporation probably have nothing to do with each other (though who can say for sure one way or the other). Your only concern is creating warning signals to alert you in advance.

GO WILD! HAVE FUN!

Creating time lines is exciting because you get feedback along the way to your prediction. As always, the trick is not to let your reasoning mind interfere but to just speak continuously.

You may find yourself speaking in the past tense. A useful perspective to adopt is to imagine yourself in the future and look backward in time from your major event to the minor ones leading up to it. Your time line then becomes a retrospective look.

Here's an example of someone speaking this January as if it were twelve months later: "In July there was an outbreak of violence in southern Russia that spilled over to the Middle East, disrupting shipping lanes in the region. Thank goodness that in April we had the foresight to start transporting our products with cargo planes. . . ."

CREATING VERIFIABLE SCENARIOS AND TIME LINES IS BASED ON THE SCIENTIFIC METHOD

The essence of the scientific method is the objective testing of a hypothesis that can be verified. A hypothesis can be verified only by making predictions: If A happens, then B will happen. Notice also that scientists "pretend" that the hypothesis is true until A occurs. Then, if A happens and B does not, the hypothesis is rejected.

We are using the same approach in applying our intuition. We treat our intuitive impressions as mini-hypotheses and then test them against each other for consistency and chronology. By linking our impressions, we set up an objective system of checks along the way with which to verify our conclusions.

~~11~~

What Is the Best Fit Between My Needs and the Market's?

(THERE'S ALWAYS A CREATIVE SOLUTION TO ACHIEVING INTEGRITY: THE *BALANCE POINT* WHERE EVERYONE WINS)

THERE'S ALWAYS A FIT

Anyone can make a living doing something he or she loves. In fact, it often holds true that you can *only* make a living in an area you find of value.

Simply find the fit. If your skills and interests are limited to basket-weaving, then use your intuition to perceive what colors and styles of baskets will be popular, what these baskets might contain to make them more marketable, and how best to market them. Add to that some good research and you're on your way to a profitable job or even the start of a profitable business.

CONSIDERING THE NEEDS OF YOUR COMPANY OR YOUR MARKET DOESN'T MEAN IGNORING YOUR OWN

Even though integrity requires us to find the balance point between our needs and those on whom our business success depends, your primary focus should always be on the former: your own. A failure to stay rooted in our own needs—and not to be so caught up in those of others in our business world—is a common reason why many people who don't like their jobs nonetheless feel "trapped." This is especially true of women.

At a certain point, a consultant I had used over the years remarked that it was odd that we could not seem to close a deal, as both my partner and I were focused on what my partner needed. She suggested I try to put the focus back on myself and the organization.

I went home that evening, and whenever I had a thought like "I wonder if he would accept . . ." or "I wonder what he really wants," I reframed my thinking by putting the focus on myself—"What do I have to do to make a deal that is solid for the organization?" "How do I keep integrity in the organization and in myself during these long negotiations?"

In a few days I noticed a shift in the balance of power now that my focus was on me and the job I had to do. I was able, by using this process, to create responsive mechanisms for the smooth running of the organization (not without some rocky moments, of course) during a time of upheaval. Many of the ideas that were implemented during that period have added strength to the organization and have made us alert, resilient, and responsive to change.

People in sales, if they're successful, usually use their intuition very well. Not only do they have to take their own temperature, they have to take the temperature of the person to whom they're selling. However, what I've often noticed with salespeople is this: Because they are so accustomed to marketing outward, they need to use intuition more in their own lives to give themselves what they want and broaden the reach and scope of their success.

It's important to use your intuition not only in your area of expertise but in your area of weakness, where you might want more help. Even in a sales situation, in an outward-marketing position, you could ask yourself, "How can I spend as little energy as possible doing things I don't want to do?" Clients will often jerk you around. Being able to intercept that behavior and redirect it is helpful to the client and to you.

Don't focus on your needs directly by asking, "What do I need in this situation?" Instead, focus first on your goal to answer the following series of questions:

- What am I selling?
- To whom?
- Over how much time?
- For how much money?

The more specific you can be with your goal, the more your intuition can help. Then you can check to see if your goals match those of your clients or prospects. That way you'll know when the right buyer comes along, and you won't even have to ask the question.

ALIGNING THE NEEDS AND VALUES OF THE VARIOUS "I's"

In chapter 5 we discussed a new framework in which to understand the different needs and values in your business world that you must satisfy. In exercise 5 (page 42) you began to record the information your intuition was providing about the values of each "I" (you, your company, your environment):

- What do you value?
- What does your company value?
- What does your market value?
- Was the language or imagery different for each of your "I's"? If so, is there the possibility of a common language with which they could communicate?
- How easy or difficult was it for you to "become" each identity?
- Did your first set of answers differ from your second set? If so, how?
- Did your intuitive answers confirm or deny your informal judgments or reasoned answers?

Refer to your journal notes for this exercise; look at your answers in the aggregate. Can all three sets of "I's" work together? If furniture were being moved, but the movers were going in three separate directions, is the furniture going to be moved? Think about it. What would you need to do to organize your "I's" into a productive system?

If too many elements in your "I's" don't fit the system, you cannot have integrity and you are working harder than you need to to promote your goals. On the other hand, when the personal, company, and environmental identities have a commonality, you can target a goal and set priorities to accomplish it.

It is hard, if not impossible, to go against the individual "I." Therefore, questions need to be conceived and worded in such a way that the individual, corporate, and environmental "I's" can have agreement.

Sometimes this requires some foresight and investigation into the possible outcome of a course of action. If you or your company is heavily

invested in selling natural products but the market is no longer interested, you might be able to focus on another element of your product
line to make the sale or create great packaging that mirrors current market trends. If you are in touch with the three "I's," the solutions are available.

Perhaps you were very invested in the idea of a promotion and your
boss's job, and now it's available. In doing the exercise, however, you
discovered a number of marketable skills you hadn't focused on before.
Do you want your goal to stay the same?

Reaching agreement among all three "I's" is especially important for
all parts of an organization. W. Edwards Deming, the founder of the
"quality movement" (and the man credited with inspiring the postwar
Japanese business revolution), said that the head of a business always
must be aware of the goals of the system. He pointed out the disasters
that can result when individual department heads pursue goals that
maximize their own return while diminishing that of the company as a
whole.

When objectives oppose each other, integrity is jeopardized and the
system becomes vulnerable. A case in point is AT&T, which had to spin
off its switch manufacturing subsidiary in order to make itself more
competitive. Companies that would normally have bought switching
equipment from AT&T were reluctant to do so because AT&T competed
with these companies in the long-distance market. A year later, business
was booming for the spin-off, Lucent Technologies, because it had
become a whole system unto itself, freed from the conflicting agendas of
its former owner.

ARE YOUR "I'S" WORKING TOGETHER?

Now that you have had an opportunity to review your three "I's," you
can identify the areas where your energy is working against you. If your
personal goal is to spend more time at home with your family, your professional goal is to be made a partner in your firm (which requires more
time at the office), and your company's goal is to employ fewer people
doing more jobs, you can more clearly define the areas of disagreement.
Now you can target your questions toward resolving and reaching your
goals in a way that maintains and even promotes the integrity of your
life and your career.

EXERCISE 11
THE ROOM EXERCISE

Imagine that you are in the center of a room. Use all of your senses to perceive yourself. As you do so, consider the following questions:

- How do you feel there?
- What are you thinking?
- What are you remembering?
- What are you hoping?
- What do you need?
- What do you have too much of?

Now, use those same senses to describe the room around you. Allow the room to develop. You don't have to "effort." Simply notice what is there:

- What is in the room with you?
- What is missing?
- Is anything out of place?
- What do you see?
- What do you hear?
- What do you smell? Taste? Feel?
- Where is there wealth?

Now, imagine yourself walking outside the room. Describe the environment and the changes as you adjust to your new surroundings.

- How do you feel?
- What do you see?
- What or whom do you encounter?
- Is there anything you left in the room that you need?
- Is there anything you brought that should have remained behind?
- As you continue on, does the environment change in any way as you observe it?

Now, return to the room. As you do so, consider the following questions. Allow the answers and information to come to you:

- Was it difficult to return here?
- What did I encounter on my journey back?
- Is the room different?
- Should it be?
- Are you different?
- Should you be?
- How would you change the room now that you have been outside?
- How would you change yourself or your habits to become a better part of this room?

Now look at your descriptions and write or speak about them for a few moments. Remember: The more you record, the richer and more useful your reading will be.

HERE'S THE QUESTION (SEE ABOVE)

"What can I do right now to create a more successful business?"

- "You" represents you.
- The room represents your company.
- The outside represents the environment that your company functions in.

The moments of transfer between you and the room, and between the room and the environment, are the contact boundaries between the integrity of the different parts of your business world.

If you do not yet have a company, an idea of what you would like to do, or even a job, you may find some answers in your responses. If you already own a company or have a job working for someone else, your responses should further clarify your situation.

For the purpose of this exercise, pretend that everything you perceive intuitively is correct. Use your other skills to make sense of it. The meaning or significance of intuitive information often reveals itself over time, so interpret it as thoroughly and carefully as you can. The nuances you perceive and interpret now may provide more guidance over time as you move closer to your goals.

ONE PERSON'S RESPONSE

My face is frozen. I am irritated. I want to scream, strike out, break free. Nevertheless, I am doing nothing.

I see myself singing and pushing myself. I see a need to love the challenge without a guarantee of success.

I see speaking on a pulpit in front of a group, like a preacher. I am motivating people to act, and they are inspired. I form a core group without having to be physically present at its core.

I smell something . . . something green? Northeastern green. I taste the soft tastes of tapioca and honey. I am deeply moved, but I am also at peace.

The room has a blue carpet.

I want to interpret everything as I write it, but I think this is a mistake. I need to give things a chance to fill themselves in.

There are people I don't want here. They need to learn to walk more softly or I need to replace them. I would want to be alone in this room simply with more gracious people.

There is a mirror on the wall that looks like a pool of water: silver, green, and blue. I feel as though I could stick my hand inside it and bring up all of the things that I want. I feel the need to focus on what I want to bring up. I keep touching the water and withdrawing my hand, empty.

There is a presence of someone who is not in the room, but needs to be either fully defined and productive or gone. I think I know who this is.

I see a tool kit on the side of the room, but the tools seem obsolete. The room has become too self-sufficient to need any tools at all.

The walls are pulsing gently. I need to bring people into the room for them to feel it. There are flowers in the room but they are a decorative cover for much more powerful methods of action. They are frames but I cannot see the pictures.

Outside seems initially gray, as if overcast, but then it turns so sunny that I cannot see. I wish I had that tool bag now because I might be able to find some sunglasses in it. The light will not burn, however; it is cool.

There are friends lining the sidewalk on either side of me. Somehow they don't know how to find me, so I hand them cards with my information on it. I don't like doing this but it is important or they will never feel the pulsing wall.

The room moves with me so that I don't ever have to go far to go back to it. It should be easy to set up and easy to tear down and move. We should fill the pictures in slowly but not focus on any one just yet. The blue color could have a hint of violet. We need to focus on bringing the outside in and the inside out.

I have sorted through the tool kit, adding some things and getting rid of others so that it can address the company's current needs. The room has to be better organized and streamlined. I need to be clearer with the people in the room about our goals and my expectations. I need to create a myth for them to live in that I want to be in, too. I need to dip into the pool and bring up an engine that works no matter where we put it.

There are too many frames distracting me from the wishing pool. I put my hand in the wishing pool and take out a smooth case. Inside lies a small key that can open any door.

I represent the room. I am the room. I need to understand that.

THE INTERPRETATION

I interpret this to mean that I need to be more active in my company and to choose a clear goal (sticking my hand in the pool and bringing it up empty). I am conflicted about doing this (an understatement!). I think that I need to take a look at that so that I can function more effectively within my company.

I need to create a "portable base" rather than the original plan of enlarging our primary office. We seem to need to return to our original product and strengthen it as well as the market's memory of it. We need to stress our product's illustrious and dependable history.

Our original product can be made more versatile (the key opens any door). This seems to come up a few times as a good focus for our energy.

I need to create an environment where people can experience our products (pulsing walls). We should concentrate less on creating new lines (the frames are there, but it doesn't seem productive to fill them).

In sum, my goal is to create a more centralized company or to become integrated as part of our history—pretty literal I would say, no imagery or metaphor here!

DISCUSSION

Your intuitive impressions and your interpretation of them will begin to reveal ways to balance the myriad values in your business world. This is no easy task, and one that changes as the various elements and their dynamics change.

EXERCISE 12
SEVEN QUESTIONS

This exercise is designed to give you more detailed information about your goal and what you need to do to accomplish it. Write down seven questions about your goal on a sheet of paper and number each one. Try for a variety that call for detail rather than simple yes or no questions.

Once you've compiled these questions, you're now going to answer them "blind." Because it is difficult for anyone to be detached about personal goals, the following technique will help your intuition respond without interference from your reasoning mind.

Here's how it works. I've listed seven questions below that correspond to your questions—though in a different order.

Record your responses to each of these questions first. Actually, what your intuition will be doing is providing information to answer *your* questions.

1. When you look up, what's the first thing you notice? Describe it in detail.
2. What is the first sensation you get in your body? Describe it in detail.
3. What is the first thing you see?
4. What is the first thing you feel?
5. What is the first thing you hear?

6. What is the first thing you taste?
7. What are you thinking right now?

When you're finished, turn to page 93 to see which of your questions your first response was referring to, which your second was referring to, and so on. Once you see the question each reading referred to, you can interpret your intuitive impressions accordingly.

ONE PERSON'S RESPONSES AND INTERPRETATIONS

READING 1: When I look up, the first thing I notice is a lamp with rectangular cutouts at the top and at the base. I am aware that I cannot see it very clearly because of its distance. I think of my friend Robert who installed it. It is over a picture representing home and family, which I never look at anymore but I love. I get the number 7 and I wonder if that is because there are seven questions. I think of words and people and all of the first initials are *J*.

INTERPRETATION: This question is about a matter that needs to be decided before I can move forward with my project. I wonder if the number 7 is July because that is around the time that a resolution would be imposed. The initial *J* is someone who I know will be involved and is not involved yet. The other imagery is appropriate for the product line for this venture. I think I may need to sort through the products or at least take a clearer look at them as there are two images about not being able to see clearly.

READING 2: I feel my body position poised and ready for action. Not nervous, just ready. I will not have to leap.

INTERPRETATION: This question is about an idea that seems to be on hold, and I was feeling impatient to get it moving in time for what I feel is our best opportunity in the market. I think I can calm down.

READING 3: I see a beautiful glass whose base looks like stone. The ice inside the glass has melted and I think that I will have to dump out what is inside and fill it with something new. I get the sense of reasoned, methodical action. The letter *p*.

INTERPRETATION: I am noticing that my initials are really good. The *p* is the name of a company that this question deals with although I know the company by another name. I understand the imagery completely. I would like to dump this now but I know that the sensible approach is to be more "slow and reasoned."

READING 4: I feel all of my aches and pains and I also know that the moment I get up and move they will go away. I feel determination. The kind of authority that what I say is unquestioned. I see an office in a very fancy district of my city. It is not mine, but I can use it whenever I please. I get the letters *c* or *k*.

INTERPRETATION: Once again my initial impressions are on target. For me this is very convincing. I believe that this is a good direction (the question) for me to go in. I wasn't sure it was. I will get more information and maybe, if the information supports it, make this my top priority.

READING 5: I hear the shuffling of papers and I feel that everything, although it sounds chaotic, is very much in order. I get a sense of ease and routine. I've found a pattern that works.

INTERPRETATION: These impressions didn't address my question as directly as did my other readings. I was asking about the chances for success of a product I am considering. This tells me that I have the routine down (despite my doubts), but I am not sure that it addresses how strong a project it will be.

READING 6: I taste a piece of hard candy I am sucking on and I want to get even more flavor from it and increase my satisfaction. I want to taste something new and that something new looks like a strawberry. I am in no hurry to get it.

INTERPRETATION: This question is about the financial rewards of my planned venture in the coming year. Looks good. I need to keep my eye on my level of satisfaction with what I am doing.

READING 7: I am thinking about how in sync I am with a friend of mine. The phone rings, but no one is on the other end. I am thinking about how the old fears no longer bother me and I have become much more action-oriented. I'm remembering my grandfather, who did things right and has imparted a great deal to me in his genes even though I did not know him well.

INTERPRETATION: I sneaked a personal question in here about how the next year would be for me. I like the picture. I was actually expecting a phone call from someone I am having difficulty with so I wonder if this means that my problems with her will end. The synchronistic thought was with my partner. That's good news. My grandfather had a very successful business and he had a lot of integrity. I think that this is a good sign for my projects. Maybe I should find out more about his company and see if there is any guidance for me in his history.

DISCUSSION

This technique can be adapted to any situation for detailed readings when you aren't sure you can give detached intuitive readings. Again, there's nothing special about the cues I chose or the number 7, though the more questions you ask in a sitting the less likely you are to "figure out" which one you are answering at any particular time.

NOW USE YOUR EMOTIONS AND LOGICAL MIND TO INTEGRATE ALL YOUR DATA

In some of the previous exercises, I asked you to suspend judgment so you would give your intuition a chance to speak. Now that you have recorded your intuitive responses, you should use what you think and know to provide a framework for your intuitive information.

ONE PERSON'S RESPONSE

When I looked at my answers to the second set of questions about my business world, I found areas of conflict between my personal needs and what my company needed from me. I also found what I think is the answer.

I need to do less busy work in the company and work more on creating a company identity that can be represented by our employees. I need to work more closely with marketing and focus less on product development.

The company has a strong need for a focal product and character that I can provide while meeting my need to not spend every minute trying to fill all the roles. I think there is a need to create short training seminars for the staff to integrate a company identity into their presentation of our products.

My goal is to create a centralized company that sustains itself on the basis of our original product. What do I need to do to achieve this?

- Strengthen and promote our original product.
- Allow myself to be more closely associated with it. Give our product and company a "personal" identity.
- Send envoys to the locations that are weaker for us to make them feel as though they have "stepped into our office" (the Northeast looks like a good place to start).
- Work on our logo and colors (blue seems to be a good one) and create consumer recognition.
- Speak more to the various uses of our product and how to acquire it.
- Create public relations opportunities that involve group efforts.
- Look at how the personnel in the office and in the field function together; weed out problems.
- Create a corporate flavor that has my values in it; develop a policy that perpetuates that culture throughout the company.

YOUR COMPLETE PERSONAL MISSION STATEMENT

In previous chapters you defined who you are and took stock of your interests. You also became your market and your team to determine their needs and values. So you've become much more conscious of what you have—and want to offer—your market. And you've done so while creating an organic whole that unites and harmonizes your needs, the needs of your team, and the needs of your market.

You're now ready to make this balance point more tangible by making a complete statement of your goal. Your complete mission statement must include not only what you're offering but who your market is and what needs it will perceive you as filling. This is what I mean by integrity. An ideal mission statement will also include some reference to the needs of your team and your environment.

Notice also that your mission statement cannot be "to make money," since it addresses neither what you have to offer nor how your market will value that.

WRITE DOWN YOUR OWN GOAL NOW

While focusing on the balance point of your integrity, write down your goal. It may change as you go farther in the intuitive process and get more in touch with your needs and those of your team and environment. That's okay. What is your goal today?

Be sure to write it down, as opposed to "keeping it in your head." The mind is a very disorderly place. If you write something down, it begins to exist. You know where to find it, what to do with it. You can take it out of the messiness of the mind.

Here are some examples of a goal or mission statement:

- I am creating meal plans for the busy professional that can be easily adapted to institutional use.
- I am creating a computer program, for use primarily by financial institutions, to evaluate the financial factors of a business deal ten times faster than existing spreadsheets and databases.
- I am creating a company that will serenade your loved one using children from the church choir.
- I am creating a stock portfolio that will enable my child to attend a private college when I retire.

Of course, although I refer to the mission statement as "personal," companies can and should have mission statements, too. If you're thinking of starting a business, your personal and corporate mission statements might be the same, but not necessarily.

~~12~~

TAKING A LOOK AT
YOUR CURRENT
DECISION-MAKING PROCESS

DECISIONS, DECISIONS, DECISIONS

Every day we are besieged by decisions in our professional lives:

- Should I pursue a graduate degree at night and on weekends or leave my job and enter the full-time program?
- Should I accept the job offer even though it means moving to a different city?
- Should I sell my mutual fund shares now and take profits, wait until next quarter to sell—or even increase my investment?
- Should I accept the promotion and pay raise, or decline it to spend more time with my family?

In this chapter we'll explore how you actually make such decisions. We'll also consider some of the serious drawbacks to traditional decision-making and ways in which using intuition—rooted in integrity—can improve its effectiveness.

Earlier I asked you to explore how you experience intuition by recalling some intuitive moments you've experienced. You also need to get in touch with your own decision-making process just as much as your intuitive one. In fact, it may be even more important since how you think you make decisions is probably very different from how you actually make them. Before you can successfully integrate intuitive information into your decision-making, you need to be more aware of how you currently make decisions.

BENJAMIN FRANKLIN ON DECISION-MAKING

Benjamin Franklin, when he wasn't flying kites, or writing *Poor Richard's Almanack,* or helping found our nation, was in the habit of dispensing his practical wisdom to anyone who would listen. This often came in the form of such catchy nuggets as "Early to bed, early to rise, makes a man healthy, wealthy, and wise." So when a friend wrote to ask him how to reach a difficult decision, Franklin offered the following advice.

Take a piece of paper and write the decision to be made at the top. Divide the sheet into two columns, one for the "pros" and the other for the "cons." Next, analyze the situation and list all the important factors in the relevant column. Then assign a numerical "weight" to each factor according to its relative importance in the overall decision; the greater the number, the greater the factor's importance.

If you're weighing three job offers, for example, you might rate the pay and benefits with a 5, promotion possibilities a 7, vacation time a 10, flexible hours a 2, and so on. Finally, tally up the figures for each column and choose whichever side has the higher score.

I don't know about you, but I'd tried to list pros and cons in this manner long before I'd heard of Franklin's approach. Oddly enough, however, I would only grow more confused.

In fact, I'd often find myself cheating! After assigning each item a number and tallying up the total for the pros and cons, I'd look at the final result and think to myself, "But I don't want to do that!" So like some disgruntled politician I'd call for a recount. I'd go back to the list and alter the individual item weights to get the result I wanted!

Franklin's model is too simple, of course. For one thing, it ignores the interdependence of various factors. In the previous example we rated pay and benefits with a 5 in importance and vacation time a 2. Well, surely, if the flexibility were great enough, or the salary low enough, you might change these ratings substantially.

Modern analytical techniques are somewhat more sophisticated. With computers and spreadsheets and databases doing the number crunching, for example, we can program the computer to take into account such interdependencies. We can even take into account ranges of values and probabilities. But all "objective" decision-making techniques are merely refinements on Franklin's approach:

- Decide on your goal.
- Establish your priorities.
- Gather and analyze the available information.
- Weigh your options mathematically.
- Tally up the scores to decide.

Does anyone seriously believe that any major successful business decisions get made this way? In our heart of hearts, we never really trust our analysis, do we? We might use this kind of decision-making to rule out obviously bad choices (like investing in a business that could never break even unless it maintained an annual growth rate of 20 percent over the next decade), or in situations that are relatively cut and dry (like choosing one credit card offer over another).

But we don't have trouble making decisions like that, do we? We need a way to make more effective decisions on the "hard calls."

DECISION-MAKING IN THE INFORMATION AGE

You're dreaming if you think decision-making is solely logical. It's a complex amalgam of thoughts, feelings, and memories, as well as intuitive impressions.

Consider the simple case of buying a car. We have our logical-rational-factual reasons: "This car gets terrific gas mileage." "It has great resale value." "The dealer's financing terms are hard to beat."

We also have our feelings and emotional reasons, many of which are unconscious: "This car reminds me of my father's." "This car will impress my neighbors."

Finally, your brain also processes your intuitive impressions (which until now have probably been primarily unconscious): "This salesman will take a cut on his commission because he's behind in his monthly quota."

This process actually provides compelling evidence for intuition's powerful role in decision-making. Let's say you are consciously aware of all the reasons in favor of something (in this case, buying a car) and almost nothing on the other side—yet still decide against it! I'm sure this has happened to you; it happens to me all the time.

Why? Because our intuition may be sending us other signals without our awareness, signals like the following: "I should postpone buying this car because a new model will be released that I will prefer." "I'm about to be laid off and I won't be able to make the monthly payments." "This new car will be stolen in less than a month."

The next exercise will help you become more aware of your current decision-making process.

EXERCISE 13
UNDERSTANDING YOUR DECISION-MAKING PROCESS

Take two difficult or complex decisions you have made in the last few years: one that turned out well, and one that turned out badly. Describe each in your journal workbook in detail. As you do so, consider the following questions:

- Did you approach them analytically first, or with your feelings, or from your "gut"?
- Did the conclusions you reached analytically agree with the ones you reached from your heart? If not, which voice—your heart or your head—did you listen to in the end?
- What internal and external conditions were going on when you made each decision? How did you feel? What was going on in your life? Where was your attention focused?
- How long did each decision take? For example, was there a long period of thought and research followed by a snap decision, or a snap decision followed by long research to back it up? Was either decision impulsive?
- Did you decide either decision by not deciding? In other words, did you let time pass and wait for events to change so that the decision was made for you?
- Did you seek the advice of others? If so, what kind of input did you seek? Did you ask them for the factors you should be considering or how to "frame" the decision, or did you ask them how they would decide?

- Did either decision come to you "out of the blue"?
- Knowing what you know now, was either decision "correct"?

Be careful on the last question. It is not easy to evaluate a decision objectively in hindsight. The temptation, of course, is to see how things turned out. That is often misleading. You can make a great decision and have things turn out badly, or make a bad decision and have things turn out well.

MAKING THE CASE FOR INTUITION IN THE BUSINESS AND PROFESSIONAL WORLD: DEBUNKING THE MYTHS

In my first book, *Practical Intuition*, I showed how anyone can get in touch with their intuition and hone it into a useful tool. Yet even "believers" in intuition are more likely to use it in their personal lives than in their professions. It might be okay, they think, to use intuition when choosing a restaurant, planning a vacation, or deciding on a mate, but it should not play a role in their professional lives. This is surprising, since the most successful individuals realize that they can't afford not to use their intuition.

Interestingly enough, one of the areas in which serious work is being done on intuitive decision-making is the military. Indeed, even Colin Powell has publicly confessed to how much he used his intuition in making key strategic and tactical decisions.

I don't mean to suggest military strategy as a business model. Like generals in battle, however, you will often be called upon to make critical decisions based on uncertain information and with little or no time to evaluate or analyze. If intuition is used—even required—in battle, surely it can be used effectively in ordinary business affairs where the stakes are so much lower.

The fact is that no matter what your career path, you already use your intuition in your professional life. Your intuitive faculty operates all the time, just like your breathing, whether you are aware of it or not. Right now, as you read these words, your intuition is operating. You can either use it well—that is, consciously—or you can use it badly.

INTUITION COMES OUT OF THE CLOSET

Intuition is used far more in the business world than is generally recognized. More and more successful individuals are admitting that they use intuition all the time in their decision-making. There are a number of reasons, however, why most business "intuitives" are cautious about publicly embracing intuition.

In the first place, the actions of executives are increasingly criticized by everyone from demanding boards of directors to angry shareholders to sue-happy plaintiffs. In light of their obligation to "be responsible" to various interests, executives must be ready to justify their decisions; it isn't easy to claim that a decision was reached "on a hunch."

Another reason that we don't hear more about intuition in the workplace is because it doesn't pay. A consultant can submit a lengthy analysis and demand far more money, for example, than one who arrived at his or her recommendation through intuition.

As a result, those who admit to using intuition tend to be entrepreneurs who are blazing new trails (remember: logical analysis provides little or no competitive advantage in the marketplace) and corporate CEOs (who admittedly can "afford" to be intuitive since presumably by the time a decision reaches their desk it has already been analyzed by several layers of management).

USING YOUR INTUITION TO GAIN AN EDGE IN A COMPETITIVE WORLD

Intuition is a way of receiving information that is not immediately present to your senses. One of intuition's most helpful elements is its ability to sense what is coming, almost to feel underneath the ground before the first rumble. Think of it as an early warning system not just for danger but for opportunities as well.

Millennia ago, individuals who followed their intuition had a distinct survival advantage over others. Intuition is the sense that allowed you to know that a rapidly approaching lion, whose arrival was beyond the reach of your five senses, was headed your way, thereby allowing you to prepare to dine on it instead of it dining on you.

In modern times, outstanding individuals have attributed much of their success to their use of intuition. This is all the more surprising in the financial and scientific worlds, fields that would seem to call solely for cold, analytical thinking. If it's good enough for Einstein and Soros, perhaps they're on to something.

One of the great strengths of logical analysis—its reproducibility—is actually one of its great weaknesses. We rely on rational analysis because we can always verify a particular conclusion by reproducing our analysis.

Unfortunately, our competitors can reproduce our analysis, too. Given the same data and assumptions, two computers will produce the same results. This may explain why investment analysts, armed with their MBAs and sophisticated analytical techniques and econometric models and Pentium-powered network computers, scarcely manage to keep up with the stock market averages!

If you want your competitors to know exactly what you are doing, rely solely on logical analysis. If you're looking for a competitive advantage, you have to go beyond the facts. You'll need to develop fluid frames of reference rather than being locked into limited conventional or traditional perspectives. Individuals as well as companies must be adaptable in the face of today's rapidly changing social, political, and business environments.

There are no new ideas or new facts, only new ways of looking at them. The world of global business—and every business today is affected by global events—is intensely competitive. You can either compete ineffectively and stressfully using only a portion of your cognitive faculties, using the same facts and analysis everyone else has access to, or you can use your intuition to see past the limiting boundaries and think "outside the box."

THE MYTH OF PURE RATIONALITY

Even though we all recognize that nobody makes decisions based purely on rational, objective grounds, almost everyone believes that he or she *should*. For the last several thousand years it has simply been taken for granted that to make our most effective decisions, we should strive to remove any last trace of emotions or feelings or subjectivity from our thinking (though, of course, this ideal would be possible only in theory).

How amusingly ironic that these same rationally minded scientists and philosophers never thought to follow their own advice and put this assumption to the test. Professor Antonio R. Damasio, head of neurology at the University of Iowa's medical school and an adjunct professor at the Salk Institute, and his wife, Hannah, also a neurologist, did. And what they discovered, published in his book *Descartes' Error*, was that this ideal leads to *terrible* decisions.

The Damasios studied patients who had suffered brain injuries to their prefrontal cortex that severed their emotional responses while their intellect, memory, and language skills remained unchanged. The tragic result was that such a person was unable to "conduct himself according to the social rules he previously had learned, to decide on the course of action that ultimately would be most advantageous to his survival, and to plan for the future"—traits, I add, that are essential in the business world. (All these individuals, incidentally, lost their jobs because they were unable to function.)

Clearly, striving to remove emotional considerations is not just impossible, it produces exactly the opposite consequences previously assumed. To be sure, strong, unchecked emotions can make clear thinking all but impossible. The question for us, then, is how we can best integrate our intuition as well as our emotion and logic.

WHAT THEY DON'T TEACH YOU IN BUSINESS SCHOOL

If you've been to business school, you were taught to believe that the world could be dissected and analyzed just like a case study. This belief is fostered by management consultants (the people who know less about your business and market than you do—except, supposedly, how to run your company). According to these "experts" (who introduce fad management theories more often than fad diets appear), running a successful business or enjoying a successful career is as simple as proving a geometry theorem. All you have to do is perform the market research, gather the statistics, enter all the data in spreadsheets and databases, and analyze the results.

What could be easier? They'll even draw pretty diagrams to demonstrate that should their assumptions be off, you'll still come out ahead ("Even if interest rates do not decline and even if your revenues fail to grow at 35 percent annually, your company can still expect to increase its market share by following three simple recommendations . . . ").

Give me a break. If things were that easy, why weren't these guys doing it themselves? It reminds me of that old saying: "Those who can't do, teach." One of the important lessons of this book is that no one can know your business as well as you because no one can know you and your needs as well as you.

TIME OUT FOR A REALITY CHECK: THE WORLD IS NOT A CASE STUDY

Why do we tend to rely so much on analysis? The simple answer is this: because it is so powerful. Logic and rational analysis have achieved incredible successes over the past thirty or so centuries since their invention, especially since the relatively modern invention of the scientific method.

In the twentieth century, the rise of ever-faster computers has allowed even more sophisticated technology and analytical techniques. So, in a sense, one of the reasons we analyze so much is because we can!

The danger is that in doing this we eliminate everything from our world that can't be easily categorized and analyzed and fit into a computer model. Our educational system is partly responsible for this trend. From grade school to graduate school, we are taught to be logical. That is okay as far as it goes.

But we are also taught that the world is logical, and that things that "don't make sense" should be ignored. Our MBAs are trained to believe that even the most complex business decisions can be reduced to simple rules. And so they are continually performing market research and feeding the results into their databases and spreadsheets and doing endless computer runs.

UNFORTUNATELY, ANALYSIS WORKS ONLY SO FAR— THEN IT BREAKS DOWN COMPLETELY

Again, logic and analysis are important, but we must not overlook their serious drawbacks. Let's consider them one by one:

- **There's too much information today to handle.** We're suffering from information overload. It has become impossible to gather all the relevant information for even the most simple decisions, and to sort the good information from the bad. What's worse, we become less decisive, paralyzed under the weight of all our information.

- **The world has become too complex.** It's fairly well agreed upon that the world has become increasingly chaotic, with paradox and change the norm rather than the exception. My brother studied physics at Harvard, and the whole situation of business executives today reminds me of the revolution created in physics a century ago by quantum mechanics and the theory of relativity. The assumptions of classical physics worked up to a point, and then broke down completely. Business executives today use twentieth-century technology and analytical techniques but base their thinking on nineteenth-century assumptions about the way the world works.

- **Gathering "all the available" information takes too long.** Someone once said that doing market research was like driving by watching your rearview mirror. By the time we've analyzed all the data we've spent so much time gathering, the world has changed. In today's turbulent times, you simply can't afford to wait "until all the research is in" before acting. By the time you've satisfied your logical, rational mind that there are valid reasons to act, it's often too late.

- **Our analysis is only as good as premises and reasoning.** In today's complex world, many of our old assumptions no longer apply. Thirty years ago, for example, many very smart people were predicting that "at current rates" the world would soon run out of food and oil. Well, we haven't run out of either. In fact, the amount of food produced per person has been steadily increasing. The problem is that we don't know which assumptions are still valid and which aren't. A big problem with analysis is that if you start from a faulty premise, the rigorous application of cold logic will lead you unavoidably to an absurd conclusion.

- **Our analysis is only as good as our information.** Even flawless reasoning can produce absurd results if the information it relies on is faulty or incomplete. Remember that information today becomes obsolete at an accelerating pace. Computer programmers use the acronym GIGO—Garbage In, Garbage Out—to describe how a computer produces bad results when "fed" bad information.

~~13~~

WHAT STEPS MUST I TAKE?
(YOU CAN PLAN FOR TOMORROW TODAY)

AS ALWAYS: TURN EVERYTHING INTO QUESTIONS FOR YOUR INTUITION TO ANSWER

Now that you have your goal, you create your plan and assemble your team (part or all of which may already be assembled) simply by asking questions.

Let's say your goal is to become king (or queen) of the universe. Even this lofty mission requires questions: How do I get there? What should I wear? Who do I know who can help me? Where will I see them? Where could I find someone today? Where could I find someone tomorrow?

And so on. By answering these questions, you will discover your plan.

Once again, you become the answer. You use everything in your body, including your feelings, your impressions, your memories, and your thoughts—to answer them.

USING YOUR INTUITION TO CREATE YOUR MASTER PLAN

Your goal should include your priorities, and your plan should reflect those priorities, too. One of your priorities might be to be the center of your family life. You'll need to organize and prioritize your resources to be able to do this.

Once you are clear on your goal and your priorities, your intuition will reveal the most direct route to your goal, unless you have a hidden agenda at odds with it. Your unconscious agenda will come through, no matter what. That's why it's so important to define your goals and set your priorities—and to do so in writing as you did in the previous chapter. They become your conscious commitment to yourself, which you begin to internalize and act on unconsciously.

YOUR PLAN SHOULD ADDRESS YOUR DEFINING QUESTIONS

In chapter 3 we began the process of establishing your mission by asking the first set of defining questions (page 29). We did this so you could establish what you wanted to offer the market—What's my greatest talent?—but we also did it so you could establish what was holding you back—What's my greatest obstacle?

Perhaps what you want to offer is not what you have. You might want to become a doctor but you don't even have a college degree, much less a medical one. Or you might want to open a restaurant but you don't know the first thing about cooking.

Your plan should address these needs. But remember that you're not in this alone. Members of your team can help you overcome your obstacles. That is, if you have a team. If you don't, your plan should include assembling one.

KNOW WHAT YOU WANT

Be clear about your objectives. If you're a broker, don't just decide to get more customers this year. Decide exactly how many more customers you want. That opens your mind to considering all the ways in which you could achieve your goal. In addition to cold-calling and direct-mail solicitations, could you co-market with other financial services professionals, like accountants or insurance brokers, by offering seminars on financial planning and expand business for everyone concerned?

INTUITION CAN ALSO HELP YOU WITH THE PLAN'S DETAILS

"I have a business," you say as a seller. "Should I sell it now or should I keep it for a year?" Or you're a real estate broker. "Should I move more into commercial rather than residential real estate?," you ask. "Would that be more appropriate for me for the next year? Do I feel the residential market going soft before there's even a sign of it? Where is my market?"

You can protect yourself as a professional by keeping your thumb on the pulse of your own profession so that you can act rather than react. Develop the ability to view situations from a different perspective and then go out and prove or disprove your information by using a combination of intuition and research.

Let's take the real estate example. Imagine that you're a developer looking at a certain piece of land. You're thinking of building a community for thirty thousand residents.

You're not sure, however, whether the zoning will be in your favor. There's some legislation in the works in a nearby neighborhood that will have ramifications for you. This legislation will specify the size of the lots, the amount of acreage that can be subdivided, how easy it will be to gain access to water, and many other critical details. In other words, this legislation will foreshadow whether this area will be attractive enough to induce people to move here and build schools, shopping centers, and churches—all the signs of a vital community.

It's important to get a gut sense about the questions you want to ask before you begin your research and analyze the details: Will the zoning that we want be passed? When? Will the county provide a new school for the area?

You'll get the answers to those questions simply through your gut.

Back Up Your Intuition with Research and Analysis

Then what do you do? Check it out. What is the normal time it takes to get zoning approved? Is anyone trying to derail my plans? Are there groups I could enlist as advocates? Does my timing make sense?

This is the time to validate all your internally generated or perceived data against reality. As always, don't just "trust" your intuition when you can verify or validate it.

If something's not in sync—if your research or analysis conflicts with your gut answers—then keep probing with further questions, both of your intuition and of whatever fact-finders you have in the real world. Don't stop asking questions until the facts and your judgments are aligned with your intuitive conclusions.

Remember: Only in rare cases should decisions be made on intuition alone.

DON'T KEEP YOUR PLANS SECRET

As with your personal mission statement, your plan can attract useful team members to your mission. If you are an individual looking for a job, you might find unexpected leads or contacts within your circle of friends or within their circles. If you are a company, you will want to attract employees who can help you realize your plan.

But this can't happen if you keep your plans in the dark. Yet most people try to keep their plans secret. I will go further and state that it's important to let as many people as possible know what your goal and plans are.

No one can help you achieve your goal and plans if they are unaware of them.

FRAMING YOUR PLAN FOR YOUR TEAM AND YOUR ENVIRONMENT

Each current and potential member of your team must see their interest in helping you with your plan and mission. In other words, the members of your team must see how helping you with your plan helps them with theirs.

Here again, it's important to frame your plan in a way that speaks to your team members.

THE FALLACY OF LONG-TERM THINKING

We are frequently told of the importance of taking "the long view" and engaging in long-term thinking and planning.

I think this is a mistake.

The problem is that people and companies engage in long-term thinking, and it's impossible to think or analyze accurately for the long-term by using only logical or empirical data. Assumptions get trashed. Events interfere. Projections become way out of kilter. Other things happen. Things change too much. You change.

Let's consider the limits of long-term planning on the corporate level since individuals usually perceive themselves as having more flexibility and adaptability. As a result of their perceived inflexibility, companies are fixated on long-term planning. They have entire departments devoted to it, armies of people crunching numbers and churning out what-if scenarios. Worldwide Widgets says its long-term goal is to control 100 percent of the automotive parts business. But the automotive business may not exist in the long term; it may even change profoundly in the next twenty years. If so, Worldwide Widgets's "plan" may blind it to other emerging opportunities. Is this a good idea? Of course not.

And what about the company that must make multimillion- or even multibillion-dollar investments based on market conditions that may or may not exist five or even three years from now when the plant is finally constructed?

AN ILLUSTRATION

Let's say you are the head of the firm that needs a new plant constructed so we can explore the typical long-term planning process. You would probably begin by looking at existing and past market indicators; perhaps you'd even poll your consumers or do some market research. Based on those findings you would do an analysis of demand. If your analysis proved that demand would increase, which for this discussion we will assume it will, you would raise funds to build your new plant.

The intuitive process would move somewhat differently. You would do all the same research, including an intuitive evaluation to see if there was anything you had overlooked. You would then focus on the question of how to increase consumer demand in the moment and evaluate whether or not, in the moment, based on all your information, a new plant was necessary. If so, you could build it, and making the plant productive would now be your current goal even before the first stone was laid.

As the plant went up you would be evaluating your market regularly so that if, indeed, the initial calculations were wrong, you would be able to respond immediately. The focus then is not on providing for something (an increased demand) which does not yet exist, but on building something in the moment to fill your goal of having enough market demand to justify your building a factory. In doing so, you might also get your shareholders or consumers excited about your plans, and you would get an immediate response, positive or negative, which you would use as information to guide you in the building of the plant, the creation of the future goal market, and so on. The focus is brought to the present.

USING YOUR INTUITION TO TARGET THE
FUTURE IN THE MOMENT

It's impossible to think long-term. You can only react in the moment. And that moment, if you're truly conscious of it, takes into account the long term, because you're responding in ways that are effective.

Having said that, it's very important to see your long-term goal daily and allow it to change. Your long-term goal is to rule the world? Hmmm . . . , doesn't feel like there's much energy there. But Mars is nice this time of year.

Intuition will bring your goal into the moment. And it will correct it in the moment. Then you can use your logic and feelings to better understand the present so that you can act on your best interests in the moment.

Ultimately, I don't think there's a big difference between short-term and long-term thinking once you've worked through the unconscious of either yourself, or the company, or both. By making yourself powerful in the short term on a daily basis, and by reinventing yourself daily, you will be powerful in the long term.

By using your intuition, you will accomplish your long-term goal in little ways in the short term. If you don't do that, you can't possibly reach your goal anyway. It's all about the moment. You can change anything and everything right now.

Intuition can take into account the long term, but it does so by responding in the moment. There's no contradiction or paradox in that. By making yourself as strong and valuable as you can be now, you're also preparing yourself for the future. Your intuition is not limited by short-term versus long-term views. If you ask your intuition whether your company should invest in a new logo, it will consider the long-term effect of such a change and respond with a yes or a no right now. Today.

If you're a buyer for Bloomingdale's and intuit that a particular style you'd like to order won't come in four months from now, you won't order that style. In the moment, you correct for long-term problems.

We may not be totally aware of it, but targeting the future in the moment is training your mind to think holistically. It's training your mind to know what the best move today will also be for tomorrow, but still making the ones that are a good move today.

Finally, doing things in the moment ensures that future problems don't occur because your intuition is really good at sensing the future. So, you can look over the parts of your company, or your plan, or your idea, or your life, and see them almost as if everything were a game of marbles. What's going to need to be addressed three months into the future? And there can be an exercise to do that.

So, in setting your priorities, the questions should define present priorities for a five-year plan that doesn't exist, because your five-year plan starts and finishes today.

INTRODUCING THE CLOCK TECHNIQUE

In many business situations it is useful to have a sense of the development of an event or a situation so that you can prepare for it. The clock technique is similar to a time line, but here you're focusing on one event rather than a sequence of unrelated events. There's nothing magical or mystical about the image of a clock face, which is simply a useful way to organize your intuitive impressions into a coherent reading.

EXERCISE 14
THE CLOCK

Imagine yourself as the center of a clock with a small hand and a big hand. On the face are circles at twelve, three, six, and nine o'clock. You may even draw a clock on a piece of paper and write in your responses if it makes it easier for you to organize your impressions.

Perceive the circle at twelve o'clock coming toward you. Notice how it moves. Notice what it looks and feels like and how those perceptions change as it moves closer.

Record any other thoughts, memories, perceptions, and observations you have, including external "distractions" and body sensations. What is your reaction to it as it moves closer?

Now perceive the three o'clock circle moving toward you. Notice the same things that you did with twelve o'clock. Ask the same questions.

Repeat the process for the circles at six o'clock and nine o'clock.

When you have finished the exercise, turn to page 115 to see what question you were answering.·

ONE PERSON'S RESPONSE

TWELVE O'CLOCK: I see two people working as a team, even though they are at odds with one another. I see a black box that is empty inside but contains dangerous secrets. I hear the song "Everybody Plays the Fool Sometimes." I go to twelve o'clock; it does not come to me. When I get there I see reassuring things that I have done in the past. They are still reassuring. The colors are green like the hills off the California coast. The old me was once at home there. I still could be.

THREE O'CLOCK: I go back to center by moving first from twelve to three. At three o'clock I receive all the jewels I could ever have wanted but I am not sure I want to bring them to the center. They are things I once coveted. Very yellow.

SIX O'CLOCK: I perceive a change in focus or residence and a rebuilding of what was old in a new way.

NINE O'CLOCK: I finally receive the instruction book now that I have figured out how everything works. I apply it to something of my own and then realize that what I invented was better in the first place.

INTERPRETATION

My reading is clear: I am starting a new career as an entrepreneur that could be at odds with my old one for many reasons. I think I need to stop defending myself against the fear that I am a "fool." This is getting in the way of my taking action.

I also think I need to make it clearer at my primary place of employment that the new venture I am starting on the side can help them. Maybe it could add clients to their roster.

I need to keep working for what I want (twelve o'clock does not come to me) and to create acceptance of my idea so that I can gain support instead of interference. I think the "black box" of my own fears has been getting in the way, along with my secretiveness about what I am doing, even though everyone knows something's doing. I guess I have structured a situation that creates mistrust.

I think my new business will be successful, but I may not want to give up entirely what I am doing at my current job. The California images and the yellow have many meanings for me. Primarily they address my desire to be in a career that has more out-of-the-office people contact. I suppose I could create some shifts at work that would help me add that to my job description.

From six o'clock and nine o'clock I am wondering if there is a way to integrate my current company and my new venture in a way that would be satisfying. I am going to rework my goal to see what comes up. Maybe the new venture could work with my current company, if I play my cards right. There would be benefits for both of us in this.

EXERCISE 15
TAKING STEPS TOWARD YOUR GOAL

Do your body check. Allow yourself to become anything—plant, animal, mineral, object—anything. Don't *try* to find something to become, simply wait until you have become it and then notice what you are.

- What have you become? Describe yourself.
- Why? What is your motivation?
- How did you become it?
- Where is it?

Turn to page 116 to see what question you were answering.

Exercise 14. You were answering the question, How is my business developing?

ONE PERSON'S READING

A computer. Quick solutions to common problems. Different files that automatically access what is needed.

I want things to be easy in the doing but complete in the results. I want to have the organizing done for me when I generate the thought.

I laid everything out on a table, sorted it, found its interrelationships, and then created segments that automatically connected to other segments.

It is in schools and generates information to be used and worked on at home.

THE INTERPRETATION

I need to create quick solutions for the difficulties that arise today instead of ponderously evaluating them for a long-term, perfect solution. I need to delegate more.

I may call a meeting and see what difficulties people are having and see ways in which we could contribute, in an immediate way, to each other's ease of functioning. I need to have my thoughts clear on how we can address the problems in specific ways. Maybe I should allow people to generate some questions to "sleep on" and bring in tomorrow.

The strange thing about this reading is it also seems, if taken literally, like a good idea for a business plan for some new products we have been developing. I think that today might also be a good day to take care of what's going on in the office in the most efficient way possible and set in motion people's ideas for the future.

DISCUSSION

The interesting thing about this reading is that once the person took care of the "noise" in the office (intuitively, at least) and reconnected the flow of ideas and energy between people and departments, a good idea and a future plan for a product line was revealed that incorporated the expertise of many departments. It led this person to question whether or not a regular "noise reduction" problem-solving meeting would generate new ideas in a more consistent and efficient way.

A woman in one of my workshops did this exercise and her information made her laugh because it told her she was supposed to be doing exactly what she was doing (all systems were go), but that she needed to remember to be wild and have a little more fun with it. She had recently started a business that was based on something that had given her a great deal of pleasure but she had forgotten to take pleasure in it.

Now you have your business world and your goal defined with integrity and you know what you need to do today to begin to build it.

Planning a Job Hunt

For the remainder of this chapter, we will apply the planning principles we've been discussing to a situation we've all faced: finding a job or getting a better one.

The Three Job Scenarios

It's always been my impression that career or job decisions fall into one of three categories:

Scenario 1:   You have no idea what to do "with your life" right now. You might also be unemployed, which compounds the problem because you don't know what area to look in to find a job.

Scenario 2:   You know what you want to do, but you're stuck in a job you don't like. Perhaps it once met your needs but either your needs have changed or the company has. You want to make a move. How can you do it?

Scenario 3:   You have a number of job offers and don't know which one to choose.

Another possibility, of course, is starting your own business, which we will consider last.

Scenario 1: You Don't Know What You Want to Do

This scenario has occupied us for much of this book because it is the hardest to tackle. By working on the exercises you may already have gotten some insight into your needs and values.

SCENARIO 2: YOU'RE STUCK IN A JOB YOU DON'T LIKE AND YOU WANT TO MAKE A MOVE

Feeling stuck may mean that you aren't aware of your options. You can either find a different job within your present company—perhaps even seeking a promotion—or you can find one outside the company. In the meantime, of course, you can try to find more value in your current position: either by reshaping your responsibilities to better meet your needs, or by reframing your needs to better meet what the job is offering.

The following exercise will help in either case and regardless of whether you move within your own company or take a job in another one.

EXERCISE 16
THE MAPPING TECHNIQUE

It is often helpful to do this exercise with both a tape recorder and pen and paper so that you can draw a map. You are going to be looking at what's going on in your job, what the connections are, and if there's any mobility.

Perceive yourself as the center of a map. Pretend to follow different directions. Follow each direction as you choose it and notice who comes to mind and what interactions are possible with those people. Notice why, and when. Notice the terrain and how it changes. Notice where you end up and how long it takes. Place them on your map anywhere that makes sense to you.

Some perceptions will make no sense at all, like "take the janitor to lunch." That doesn't matter. You want to move this process from your internal sight or senses to something external that you can examine and act on.

Use our techniques to hop mentally into each person you encounter on your paths—always with your point of view as the perspective—get an idea of who's moving where, what they are focusing on, if that's a productive area for you. Do you see a wall? Is there any way around it? If not, turn back.

Make your map time-sensitive as well. This is today, this is two weeks from today, and so on. Include what you are intuiting from the outside. What is in your sphere of influence? What is outside it? How can you bring the outside in? Where do you need to spend your energy?

We spend much of our mental energy on what is outside our sphere of influence. Avoid doing this. You've got to know what surrounds you in order to be able to work with it, but you don't have to become involved in it. Your intuition can show you what will be around so that you can prepare yourself to receive it or defend against it. Chaos can burn up your energy if you're not prepared for it, or it can be highly creative when it's contained. Your goal, of course, is to focus your energy in the directions that will be most useful to you.

Start asking yourself questions: Where should I be? Where do I want to be? Is there any way to move there? Whom do I go to? Do I begin a move outward, which may mean out of my company, in order to better reach my goal?

Begin to draw patterns. Literally, you are making a map.

PERHAPS YOU ARE TRAPPED BY YOUR HIDDEN AGENDA

Another explanation to explore seriously is the following question: Is it possible that although you don't like your job consciously, it satisfies your hidden agenda?

Finally, you may feel stuck in your job because you're afraid to move. If this applies to you, I would be more concerned about the risk of remaining in a job that stifles your needs.

WHY WAIT FOR WANT ADS WHEN YOU CAN BE PROACTIVE: INVENT A JOB FOR YOURSELF

Let's say that you work in the back office of a global bank. You install the voice technology that allows data to be entered into computers by voice rather than keyboard strokes. You've done the mapping exercise. Through the intuitive insights it provided, you sense that a number two marketing position has been created in the bank's new electronic commerce subsidiary. You want that position. Internet technology is hot, and that job would get you out of the back office and into the action.

Your next step, having first exercised your intuition, is to get as much substantiating information as possible. Remember the importance of verifying your hunches: You always want to get hard data before you make a move. Take someone to lunch from the new subsidiary so you can confirm what you already know intuitively. Ask relevant questions: When will the new product be launched? Are any customer trials now in progress? Has any research been conducted? What were the results? Are any customers already lined up to use it? What have been the biggest problems so far? What will be the biggest challenges over the next year? Who are the key competitors? How is the product better than or different from its competitors'? What skills are they seeking for this first group of hires?

Armed with this information, your challenge is to come up with a creative way to sell this new venture on why it needs someone with technical skills in a marketing spot.

Frankly, you could "invent" the reason and then find the facts to justify it. There's nothing "underhanded" in this. In fact, we do it all the time. We make choices and then go back and justify why they were the right ones. I'm suggesting you do this process proactively rather than reactively so that you can give yourself more opportunities to control your destiny.

For example, you could tell this new subsidiary that your technical skills are especially strong with regard to the human-machine interface, which is the essence of electronic commerce. Furthermore, based on your experience in getting computers to work when spoken to, you can develop a series of models that will allow customers to interact with computers and determine the level of savings they could achieve by using electronic rather than paper-based commerce. Could you do this? Yes! Have you ever done it before? No! Did you just make it up on the spot? Of course! But your response came from your intuition. And isn't that response a whole lot better than saying you are "a geek who talks to computers"?

What you've done is translate your skills as an X specialist into what's needed as a Y manager. Consciously or not, you've reviewed your assets and noticed the person within you that you needed to be to secure the new job.

Scenario 3: You Have a Number of Job Offers But Don't Know Which One to Choose

Isn't this a great "problem" to have? Here the question becomes, Which of these jobs will I find the most satisfying?

You'll have to define satisfaction to formulate the question precisely enough:

- What precisely does not satisfy me?
- Do I feel there's not enough heart in my work?
- Do I think I'm not making enough money?
- Do I want more control?
- Do I want to try a leadership position?

At this point you'll narrow your selection down to a few positions, at which point I recommend our dependable old envelope method (page 54). Prepare a written list of questions beforehand so that you are getting comparable information about each opportunity as well as the random information that your intuition will generate. Here are the kinds of questions you should ask:

- What names come to mind that I should make special contact with regarding this job?
- Which "me" do I need to be for these people and which of my qualities are most attractive to them in terms of their hiring me (you don't want to get a date instead of a job)?
- What possible difficulties will this job present for me?
- Which possible difficulties or dissatisfactions will I present for them?
- When would they need to hire me (or alternatively, when would be the best time to approach them)?

Do not look at your answers until you have completed all of the envelopes.

Finally, remember to compare your intuitive hits with what you know and have researched about each position.

ADAPT THE TOY EXERCISE

We used the toy exercise (page 64) to get in touch with what we truly wanted to do. You can adapt it to this scenario by asking which of the following jobs would make this child most happy.

STARTING A BUSINESS THAT'S RIGHT FOR YOU

The other alternative, as I mentioned earlier, is not to find a job but to start your own business. The questions you need to ask yourself are fundamentally the same. The big difference, of course, is that you are taking your destiny in your own hands. The advantage, of course, is that you will not have to compromise the integrity of your needs in the least: You've created a job position completely molded to you and your values.

DON'T FORGET TO INTEGRATE YOUR INTUITION

Remember that while this is a book about developing and using your intuition, it is just one aspect of your decision-making process. As always, you will consider the same questions in all these exercises by using logic and your emotions.

~~14~~

Maintain "Distance"

It's Important to Keep Your Logic, Emotion, and Intuition Distinct

This is easier said than done. Your brain is an information processing machine far more complex and sophisticated than any computer. You don't have to "do" anything for this processing to take place. Every second of every day, you are continuously monitoring your internal as well as your external environment. Your brain then automatically combines all the information provided by your five senses and your intuition, along with your thoughts and feelings and memories, to give you conclusions and tell you "what's going on."

As a result, it can be very hard for us to tell the difference between one form of input and another. That, in turn, muddies our thinking. But it also prevents us from using each one—logic, emotion, and intuition— as a check against the other. One way to check your intuitive conclusions is to compare them with your logical and emotional ones. Incidentally, you should expect some disagreement. Your intuitive conclusions are probably suspect if they are completely in sync with what your logic and emotions tell you!

Intuition First, Then Logic, Then Emotion

Your goal is to train yourself to respond to a question first with intuition, then with logic, then to get a grip on how you feel emotionally about the question. Again, that's the ideal; unconsciously these processes will be going on without your direction. The important thing to strive for is to keep your logical, reasoning mind at bay long enough for your intuition to have a crack at the problem.

Notice that this order is completely different from the conventional model of the creative process. The accepted wisdom is that you should immerse yourself in all the available information on a problem and then attack it head-on with all the logical and analytical tools you have at your disposal. Only when you have exhausted your analysis should you "let the problem go" to "allow your intuitive unconscious" to come up with the solution. Sooner or later the solution will come "out of the blue, when you least expect it." Many celebrated scientific discoveries are said to have been made in this way.

The problem with this approach is that once your rational, logical thinking has gotten hold of a question or a problem, it becomes like a hungry dog that has sunk its teeth into a bone—it doesn't want to let go. Because we've become trained over the years to approach things analytically and ignore our instincts, the reasoning process easily overwhelms your intuitive impressions as well as how you interpret them.

THE LESS YOU "KNOW" ABOUT SOMETHING, THE MORE YOU'LL NOTICE YOUR INTUITION ABOUT IT

So, how can we allow our intuition to work without interference from our reasoning mind? One effective way—especially for beginners—to stop the reasoning mind in its tracks is to cut it off completely from any kind of information. For beginners to notice their intuition, it's best not to have any kind of information.

This is the major purpose in your learning how to do "blind" readings. One reason we don't consciously use our intuition more often is because we usually have so much information "to work with."

Here's an example of how quickly, with the least prompting, your reasoning mind intrudes itself. You're going to an important meeting with someone you don't know. This is a common business situation, from going on a job interview to selling something to a new customer.

Now, if you give your mind the least clue about this person—even a name—your brain's impressive logical apparatus swings into operation before you know it! Let's say the person's name is Goldberg. Almost instantaneously your reasoning brain reaches back into its memory bank and paints a picture of this person by using assumptions and unconscious associations based on past experience.

So you already "have an idea" not only of this person's needs, values, likes, and dislikes—but where he grew up, his appearance, his age range, even his habits. It would be one thing if our brains treated these conclusions as the most tentative of assumptions, but in practice they almost instantly get "recorded" as "facts."

You're more than a little surprised, then, when you're introduced to Whoopi Goldberg, *Ms.* Whoopi Goldberg. I'll bet I caught you. Did you find yourself getting an idea of "Mr. Goldberg" even without my prompting?

Instead of this scenario, what I'm recommending is that you record your impressions before you know anything about the person. Knowing "anything" means anything! Seeing even a picture of someone for a second is enough to give your analytical mind all kinds of visual information based on the person's face, clothing, and body language; the sound of another person's voice over the phone also reveals an incredible amount of information.

Again, once you've recorded your intuitive impressions you can and should use your logic and emotions to see what new information they provide.

━━━━━

DAILY PRACTICE
WHAT'S MY LINE?

Do you remember the old television game show *What's My Line?* The celebrity "panel" was given a brief description of a particular person's unique occupation or skill. They were asked to identify which of the three contestants he or she was by asking each one a series of questions that called for detailed answers. The ringers, ordinary volunteers, were always surprisingly good at improvising plausible responses.

This exercise was inspired, in part, by this show. The twist that we're going to make is that we can't ask any questions. In fact, we won't know anything about the person.

Before you meet someone new—and you can do this on the spur of the moment—get a quick hit in I-mode on this person: What does he need?

What is he afraid of? What would he like to hear? What in my background would he most relate to?

Remember to do this before you even have a name "to go on." If someone schedules your appointments, tell this person to give you only the times, not the names, until you ask for them.

<center>~~~~~~</center>

OTHER WAYS TO POSTPONE YOUR ANALYTICAL MIND

In addition to blind readings, you have already had a lot of practice with another technique that achieves much the same result: speaking continuously during your readings. By speaking "off the top of your head" you don't give your reasoning mind a chance to butt in.

Another effective technique is to create a symbol or metaphor for your "target" and do your reading based on this substitute. The symbol you choose is itself an intuitive hit and helps distance you from your subject whether it's a person, a company, a product, an event, or a situation.

LET'S NOT FORGET KEEPING EMOTIONAL DISTANCE, TOO

Logic is not the only thing that can interfere with your intuitive process. The techniques we just discussed serve equally well to prevent your emotions from "clouding" your impressions.

You're talking with a friend and business associate when he asks you whether you think he'll get the job promotion he's been working so hard for. Your intuition is trying to tell you that not only will he not get the promotion, he's about to get sacked!

Unfortunately—from an objectivity standpoint—you have feelings for this person. You wish him well. You know how hard he's worked and you want him to get that promotion almost as much as he does.

These strong emotions easily override not just your much subtler intuitive sense, but even whatever insights your logic might have been able to offer. This all takes place in a heartbeat, and your instant reply is, "Absolutely! I'm sure you're going to get that job." You're not lying, at least not consciously. You *are* sure. You're sure because your emotions have completely overshadowed your intuition and your logic.

REMINDER

Intuition first, then logic, then emotion.

THE IMPORTANCE OF REMAINING DETACHED

To give accurate readings and keep your thinking clear, you need to strive for a detached perspective. In addition to the techniques we've already discussed (blind exercises, speaking continuously, creating symbols), there are two other methods to help you remain objective.

The first is to know in advance the outcomes you want to avoid, and then entertain the possibility that you can handle even these unpleasant situations. I was never a good softball player because when the ball looked like it was going to hit me, I'd close my eyes instead of ducking. You always have choices.

The second is to realize that any particular outcome is negative largely because of our limited knowledge and perspective. Some things are clearly terrible no matter what perspective we take. But apart from these obvious tragedies, we can never be sure. We often assume an event is bad or unfortunate when it might have been the best possible thing that could have happened.

Your friend's losing his job, for example, might pave the way for an even better job somewhere else. Or an entirely new career. Or more time with his family, which was his hidden agenda.

There's simply no way of knowing.

With practice, you'll learn how much detachment and perspective you are able to get on the subject of an intuitive reading if you know who or what the subject is. You will eventually develop a placement of attention that allows you to view the subject with detachment when doing an intuitive reading.

EVERYTHING I'VE SAID GOES DOUBLY TRUE WHEN YOU'RE DOING A READING FOR YOURSELF!

Usually, the target about which we have the least objectivity is ourselves. You can reread this chapter to reinforce the main points as they refer to personal readings.

~~~~~

DAILY PRACTICE
FINDING THE SILVER LINING

It's one thing to understand "in your head" that apparently negative outcomes may in fact be blessings in disguise, but it's another to realize this deep
down in your heart and soul, in your unconscious. So from time to time conjure up situations that at first glance might seem undesirable for someone—
or yourself!—and practice both your ability to deal with it and to recognize
the hidden positive potential.

~~~~~

~~~~~

AN INTUITIVE TALE

It was 1976 and I was working at Citicorp as its director of training.
My career to that point was nothing special; I was hardly on the
fast track. I would describe myself as an "Okay-let's-roll-up-our-
shirtsleeves-and-get-this-job-done" kind of guy. I had achieved my
middle-management-level position in human resources through
competence and teamwork. Because almost everything I did was
people-oriented, I'd learned to rely heavily on my "gut" sense of
what's right, what will work, what feels good inside.

My life dramatically changed that year when the head of
human resources assigned me the task of developing the "best"
people management education program that had ever been done
at Citicorp. I knew a lot would be riding on how well I met these
lofty expectations, a realization all the more daunting because I
had never taken an executive development program before.
Clearly, I was being stretched.

The first thing I did was to surround myself with the best
training development people available, hired a consultant, and
went to see what other companies were doing. Based on their
exhaustive research and brainstorming efforts, my team put
together a program design and submitted it for my final approval.

I spent several hours thinking about the program's design and
imagining how it would roll out in practice. It certainly seemed

well-conceived and comprehensive, including lectures, seminars, case studies, and role-playing exercises.

But my gut instinct told me something was missing. I imagined myself in the class and kept feeling that somehow the program wasn't addressing my personal needs. As a participant, I wanted the course to help me focus on what I needed to learn, what would make me a better manager.

I asked myself how we could accomplish that. Then, suddenly, in my mind's eye I saw each student walking away from the course with something different and uniquely his own. I also sensed that the program was "spiraling."

The solution was quite easy. We simply added a feedback component in the preliminary questionnaires: "What do you expect to learn in this course? What do you think would be helpful to learn? In what ways do you think you could improve as a manager?"

This feedback would then serve as the focus of each student's learning. Each person was allowed to tailor the program's focal point to his or her own perceived concerns. Of course! And when I thought about this feature, everything else fell into place and the entire program made sense. I just knew this feedback would make a difference, I felt it would make a difference, and I intuited it would make a difference.

The feedback component became the distinguishing feature of my final recommendation to my boss. The program was immediately implemented and became an instant success. "Managing People" went on to become the most popular human management course of its kind at Citicorp. Since its introduction it has been used by hundreds of thousands of employees around the world.

❧❧❧❧❧

~15~

How Can I Best Present Myself and What I Am Offering?

(TO SELL YOUR PRODUCT, OR SERVICE, OR SKILLS, YOU HAVE TO "SPEAK" IN A LANGUAGE YOUR MARKET UNDERSTANDS AND RESPONDS TO)

COMMUNICATING ONE-ON-ONE: THE KEY TO SALES AND NEGOTIATIONS

Often, the way you "frame," or present, information helps the other person or company accept it and therefore work more efficiently. The same holds true for your company or your market. How many employees have willingly accepted pay cuts to save the jobs of their coworkers? These same employees may have gone on strike for pay raises a few years earlier. Same issue. Different context. Different outcome.

Let's consider a real estate example. If you sense that a certain client needs to know certain things, you can steer the conversation away from nonessentials. It certainly helps in terms of knowing the property and solving what little easy-to-fix problems could fetch you a significantly higher asking price. And if your intuition tells you that your clients are "just looking" and don't intend to buy for a year, you might want to add them to other clients you're showing around rather than focus a great deal of attention on them.

You're the real estate agent. You know that the walls on a building need some work and that there's a good chance the buyer will notice this and not even consider the property. So you say, "The walls need some work. We've done an estimate. It will cost about $3,000 to repair.

The sellers are happy to do it, or we can subtract it from the offering price." You've been honest and taken care of the objection up front, clearing the way for the buyer to focus on the property's good points. The way you present information to a client is essential.

A lawyer friend of mine had to go to court one day and she thought she was going to lose, so she asked me what I thought would happen. I reframed her question immediately as, "How can I make a successful outcome happen?" I wanted her to listen to their arguments but not allow them to throw her. Even though their arguments would be very logical, I knew her main point could overcome their logic and the result would be like dominoes falling.

So I told her, "You are going to ignore all their arguments and give them yours as a response, so that it all goes down like a house of cards."

And that's exactly what she did. I prepared her without telling her what she would be tempted to do, because that would have made her nervously focus on not addressing each argument instead of focusing on what she could do to make her argument work.

To tell her the truth exactly as it came to me would not have served her.

QUICK-HIT COMMUNICATION EXERCISE

The following exercises will help you respond instantly and instinctively to another person's communication needs.

- The next time the phone rings, before you pick it up and know who's on the other end, notice what you're perceiving (body check) and then target some questions: Who is it? If you're unsure, is it someone you know? Why is he or she calling? You can also ask I-mode questions: What is this person's biggest obstacle? What is his or her mission?

  Not only will you be surprised by how often you know who's calling in advance, your conversations will be richer and you'll have a greater feeling of connection with your caller.

- Here's an Internet version of the previous quick hit. Before you look at your E-mail, see if you can sense how many messages are there. See if you can sense which one you need to address first, or if any of them are important. Where is it in the lineup? Who is it from? What does it concern?

- If you're walking down the street, get a quick hit on which one of your friends or associates you'll meet first. What will he or she be wearing? What will he or she say to you first?

- You're on your way to a meeting although you don't know who will be attending. How many people will be there? What is each person's primary and hidden agenda? Which person should you address first? What should you ask or say? How will that person respond?

Whenever you have an encounter of any kind, you'll find that you receive valuable information about who you're dealing with and what's on their mind.

EXERCISE 17
READING PEOPLE

Pick three people with whom you will be speaking today and ask yourself how each will respond to the question "How was your day?" Allow your answer to be brief and immediate.

When you speak to these people, ask them this exact question and compare their responses to your intuitive ones.

Note that how they report it may be different from how their day actually went. Again, be precise. Check with them at the end of the day and compare their responses with your intuitive impressions. You will learn your "good, neither, or bad" response by practicing in this way, and that is the response most often needed in split-second decisions.

Try this exercise. It may feel odd, so I ask that you pretend that it will work. I think your results will convince you.

WHEN IN ROME—SPEAK ITALIAN

When negotiating any kind of goal it is essential to be aware of and be able to respond to the other person or company's language. By language I mean how they express and interpret themselves, their needs, and their philosophy. You need to be consistently aware of your goal while conveying it in a "language" they will find acceptable.

I recently had the experience of taking my precious son, whom any school should be happy to have, to be interviewed by schools for the very few places in each one allowed to new students. I knew that for schools above Sixty-fifth Street a button-down or polo shirt was in order and jeans were out. For the downtown schools, his mix of Terminator and Winnie the Pooh was just fine. Uptown, shake hands; downtown, say hi and shake hands if you feel like it, but his own salutations, "High five, man," or "Hey," were very marketable.

My son is comfortable in both environments and in "being" both people. But I knew which of him he had to be to achieve our goal of having the school see him as one of them. My son, by the way, is five. That his "first choice" also chose him is no coincidence: The school is a perfect fit.

It was interesting to me that as a parent I gave my son guidance on how to market himself. But it was he who said, "I like this place," and made his choice (I heartily agreed). He had chosen the school that spoke his language of curiosity, community, and commitment, and who showed it to him. The school, in turn, had attracted a student who shared its values.

STAYING IN TOUCH WITH YOUR MARKET REQUIRES INTUITION

Earning a profit—and maintaining your integrity—means sensing your market's needs and presenting what you have to offer in a way it will perceive as meeting those needs. Business, in short, consists of your selling and marketing what you have to offer, whether it's an idea, or a toaster oven, or a stock portfolio.

Always remember that "your market" is not some huge demographic but flesh-and-blood human beings. And sometimes you interact with your market one-on-one.

If you are to succeed in the business world, you must know not only what that person needs but the language he speaks.

What complicates matters is that communication occurs on many levels, most of the time unconsciously, and that the language of needs is not words and numbers and logic—but irrational desire. We often make the mistake of addressing the logic rather than the desire, but logic has no juice. The best manipulators ignore logic and address desire. They leave it to the other person to find the logical background to substantiate what it is they want.

EXERCISE 18
WHAT CAN I DO FOR YOU?

First, become aware of your judgments. For example, what do your instincts tell you before you meet a client?

Let's say a client has just called your office. Before you call him back, take a moment to write down your impressions:

- Do you feel nervous? Calm?
- Have you ever felt this way before?

Now focus on your client:

- What is he looking for?
- How does he need to feel in order to be a good buyer?

Begin writing down all your perceptions. Then allow to come to mind from all your faculties what you think is perfect for him. Ask him questions covering the typical client concerns—but ask them of yourself also:

- What's the upper limit of his budget?
- What would induce him to spend that?
- What is he looking for? What does he want to avoid?
- How do I as a professional need to approach this person?

Before you call him back, get all that information down on paper. It should take only a few minutes. Just notice everything you're feeling, or sensing, or seeing, or hearing, what you're selecting to be aware of, after you ask yourself the question, "What do I need to make this a good client for me?"

ONE PERSON'S EXAMPLE

I don't feel like making this call. It's not a good time for my client; maybe it's not a good time for me. Later today, I feel positive about making the call.

I want to remember to ask him if this is a good time to speak. I feel that this is someone who respects courtesy and doesn't mind the extra time that courtesy takes. When I focus on what he's looking for I see that he wants something small and easy to manage. Probably a better co-op candidate than a condo. He feels like a first-time buyer who needs to be reassured about the steps he needs to take in buying a home, as well as their simplicity.

I feel that he wants something for under sixty thousand dollars, but he's not sure what he can get for that amount. He cares more about where the property is located in terms of convenience than the qualities of the property itself. He wants to avoid anything that takes upkeep and any restrictions on freedom, such as a doorman. I feel as if someone else has counseled him to buy something and that he is not totally convinced. He needs to see that it will be as easy as renting.

I should show him the middle and upper level of his price range; since he really doesn't care about the place itself, he could choose to spend the least amount of money and buy something that he will later be unhappy with and that I will get less commission on. If I keep things simple, this should be a quick sale.

<hr />

DAILY PRACTICE
SENSING THE PRICE GAP

People need to notice the distance between two things. The next time you go grocery shopping, go to the produce section and pick out some lettuce. I want you to sense intuitively how much the store is netting on each head of lettuce (or pound of onions or whatever).

If you learn to think this way intuitively, when you make an offer on a product, you'll be able to feel instinctively the distance between the offer and what's acceptable. And you need to feel that space if you're going to have room to maneuver.

This skill comes in handy when you're buying a house, for example, because you will be able to feel the distance between the asking price and what you'd like to pay. That knowledge, in turn, will help you figure out how to get the price you want. And if you don't think you can figure out the grocer's margin on a head of lettuce? Then make it up, pretend you can do it.

Practice this exercise as often as possible to develop a feel that will come in quite handy in any negotiation. The more you practice, the more accurate you'll become, but the object of this exercise isn't merely to be right. It is to open up that part of you that senses so you can begin to sense and respond to the underlying dynamic behind interpersonal relations.

THE MESSAGE IS ALSO YOU

The message you are communicating to the marketplace is framed not just by the language you use but by your personality. Although psychology stresses the integration of "self," I often wonder if we don't undermine some of our greatest strengths by trying to integrate them into a coherent personality. On the other hand, I agree that our integrity needs to be at the base of all of the personae we use.

Are you the same person in the bedroom as you are in the boardroom? If so, you hold a very tough meeting but are a terrible lover. You have many distinct, albeit incompletely formed personae, any one of which can be helpful to you in the right situation.

EXERCISE 19
ESTABLISHING YOUR PERSONALITY REPERTOIRE

Right now, make a list of a few personalities you have. A sure way to illustrate and enter into this exercise is to think of who you are when you are with your mother and who you are when you are with a friend. How would each of them describe you?

Here's one person's repertoire:

- Nicely mannered Southern boy with a good knowledge of current events. I am polite and deferential to my elders and am a good audience.
- Romantic and incredible dancer with an extensive knowledge of wine. I am a free thinker and an adventurer. Generous to a fault, and gifts are always in the best of taste.

- Tough negotiator. I can walk away from any deal, and will. People have to work hard to get my interest and to keep it. Very East Coast Ivy League.
- Loyal friend, reliable in any emergency. I always give good advice. I am objective, but I will always stick by a friend even when the person is in the wrong. I require loyalty.
- Loving partner. I really try to help my partner realize her ambitions. I can be irritable, but I never hold a grudge. I will do anything to help make my partner's life better. I am direct and very much the "head of the household."

It's helpful to know your repertoire in advance so you can intuitively use one or more of your personae to respond productively to a situation. People get stuck in one behavioral model, the personality that has proven the most effective in most situations. Sometimes it's necessary to break a pattern.

By allowing yourself to be more conscious of the many "you's," your intuition can help you choose the best "you" to put forth to respond to the question, "Who do I need to be right now so that I can create the best result in this situation?" Another way to identify "who" you need to be in a given situation to get the best result is to notice which one of your friends pops into your mind and allow that to be an intuitive cue that you need to employ some of the qualities you admire in that person in your current situation.

EXERCISE 20
USING YOUR PERSONALITIES

I'd like you to look at three different interactions you're going to have today: one personal, one creative, and one financial. Don't get too complicated here: The personal one could be whether to change your hairstyle, the creative one deciding what to prepare for dinner, and the financial one wondering whether to wait for an upcoming sale.

Once you've chosen these three interactions, decide which of your personalities is offering what, withholding what, and so on.

VIDEOTAPE YOURSELF!

I strongly recommend that you photograph or videotape yourself and really examine the pictures for clues about your one-on-one interactions. Who knows, your hair, or your dress, or your body posture may be a great calling card.

Really, do this. At the very least, have an associate take a snapshot of you without your knowing. You'll be amazed at what it reveals about how your personalities present themselves to others.

COMMUNICATING TO GROUPS: SENSING THE NEEDS AND AGENDAS AT MEETINGS

Let's define meetings as any gathering of more than three people in reference to your business. The situation is not fundamentally different from the one-on-one situation we just reviewed in terms of your needing to stay focused on your needs as well as the needs of the "other side," and how you must frame your objectives in a language the "other side" will accept.

The difference in meetings, of course, is that the other side consists of many agendas, and usually there's less time for you to observe objectively or analyze consciously. And instead of "being" one person, you must now extend your intuitive awareness to many.

PREPARING FOR FUTURE MEETINGS WITH A FANTASY PREVIEW

Sometimes you won't know when a meeting is going to occur; what you do then is to make a time line. So from now until, say, December, you can lay out your meetings month by month.

This would be the case if you're just starting a job or a business, because you don't have any meetings scheduled. You might want to consider when your first interaction will occur. And if you don't see one occurring, you can ask yourself how you can create one.

See yourself at a distance and then allow your intuition to suggest how many people will be at that first meeting. Whom are you drawn to? Why? Perhaps you get the sense of a bald man, and that you were drawn to him because he was trying to cover up an overexpenditure.

This is the first thing that pops into your mind. Who is your attention drawn to next? Perhaps your attention is drawn to a blond woman.

Again, you turn that into a question: Why? Aha! She knows about the cover-up and she intends to expose him at the same meeting.

Again: Every time you notice something, ask yourself why, why am I focusing on this?

And now you sense you're focusing on these matters because you only have three days in which to make a decision.

And so on. The point is to fantasize. What you're allowing yourself to do is scan the future to see what draws your attention, and then to ask yourself why. If it's a threat—something that goes against your goals and needs—how do you see yourself neutralizing it? And then in neutralizing it, how do you bring it around to what you need?

In this hypothetical meeting, for example, I would bring the integrity back to my need by saying that I need to address both his cover-up and her attack. "There's been a lot of financial disorganization going on, but we're not going to address that in any way at this meeting today."

I've been assuming in this fantasy that I called the meeting. So if I imagine that I'm not heading the meeting, I might seize the floor at the first opportunity by saying, "I have Project Number One, which we have seventy-two hours to complete, and may I take twenty minutes at the beginning to get everybody's hit on this before we go on to further issues?"

Either I'll be granted that request or not. If not, then I'm aware that this confrontation is going to take place, and I can now direct my attention to other people within the group for an ally to be able to help me get my needs met.

The fantasy preview is almost like a radar system. We are getting information through this "radar" all the time, but we often act upon it without recognizing either the information or our goal. I often notice this "system" at parties to celebrate important events.

Everyone has a common goal, which is to make the party a success, and without being consciously aware of it, the guests will intuitively bring something that the host forgot, or will put on upbeat music when someone who is depressed arrives.

Try picturing your fantasy of your next meeting. Remember that the more literal the picture, the less accurate it is. If we're being logical and intuitive at the same time, our intuition suffers, because we're schooled in logic.

You can do this fantasy preview for a meeting next week or a meeting in the distant future. The important thing is to fantasize not only about who will be attending the meeting but also about what their agendas are and how you will maintain your integrity by focusing on your goal.

GETTING A QUICK TAKE ON THE SITUATION

Even if you don't know in advance the people you'll be meeting, and haven't had the chance to preview the situation, surprise yourself. Intuition says that the information is there, accessible to you in the moment, and that you've noticed more than you think you have.

As soon as you enter the room, immediately look around and get quick hits of every person. What are they doing? What are they wearing? How are they sitting? As you are doing this, allow your intuition to give you a key word or sense about what to expect and how to respond to each person. Your intuition will notice what you need to know.

When you sit down, keep your goal in mind and allow your intuition to provide insight, moment to moment, on how you should behave, what to expect, and how to respond. Stay focused on your agenda, then take stock of what the other agendas present could be.

Another thing you can do at a meeting to take the pulse of the various parties and their relationships—and this is a technique I often use— is to make a dot for each person and then draw angles between the dots, letting your intuition guide you as to where to draw the lines. The lines tell you where the energy is going and who is connected to whom, whether they realize it consciously or not. The lines also make you aware of the connections that need to be made. As far as anyone else at the meeting is concerned, you're simply doodling on your legal pad.

INTRODUCING THE TENTACLING TECHNIQUE

Tentacling is another way to organize intuitive information when there is more than one object that must be looked at simultaneously, in the moment, to manage a situation. Clearly, this is usually the case at meetings. This technique is particularly good for ferreting out hidden agendas.

If tentacles don't work for you as an image, choose another. You can use lines and dots, as I mentioned earlier. The meeting participants' shirt colors are another good image. Or names. Or numbers.

You can also use a clock image to predict the progression of a meeting or a deal, a plan or an event. By having some feeling for the progression of events and possible delays or issues that might arise, you can deal with them in the present and avoid potential difficulties.

The point is to feel the pulse of people's movements by whatever tactic works best for you. As you become more expert at this, you will be able to predict their movements and intercept them in a productive way.

EXERCISE 21
TENTACLING

List three people with whom you have dealings on a regular basis. Imagine all three of them in a room with you. Now, pretend you are an octopus and have a tentacle around each of the people.

Focus on your goal, which is, say, to create engagement and agreement on a course of action. Then think of some questions for each person:

- What does this person need right now to create agreement?
- What does this person need right now to be defused?
- What does this person want?

Ask yourself to notice what "I" questions come to mind and answer them:

- Who do I need to be in this moment to achieve the goal?
- What position could I take that would resonate with all these people and promote my goal?

Keep your tentacles in place throughout the meeting to note and respond to any changes.

Successful traders use this technique with the market, whether or not they do so consciously. They keep a tentacle around the world environment, a tentacle around the companies they are trading with, and a tentacle around their competition. They become the heartbeat of their subjects. In this manner they are alerted to any subtle changes in the pulse of the economic environment that would affect their trades.

STAY FOCUSED ON YOUR GOAL

As with all intuitive work, it is essential to identify your goal and the targets for intuition that bear watching to achieve that goal. An easy image is one in which you are taking a constant pulse on the factors that affect you so that you are alerted to any change that could threaten the integrity of your goal.

Let's say you're in a meeting whose purpose is to name a new cereal. You're especially fond of the name Bing Bongs. Suddenly Rick, the product manager, turns to you and says, "That's a silly name!"

Instead of getting distracted from your agenda, you pause for a moment before responding and immediately send out a tentacle to him (if you haven't done so already). Having gotten a hit of Rick's needs, you know how to frame your reply.

"The reason I like the name, Rick, is because Bing Bongs reminds me of an open land like Kansas and kids playing with cans in a field."

Presto! Rick becomes an ally. Why? Because Rick comes from Kansas and that's what he did as a child. You didn't read his résumé to realize that (and childhood games wouldn't have been on it anyway). Your intuition told you that.

Later, of course, you check out his objection through focus groups. Intuition won't always get rid of an objection, but it will cause it to surface sooner and turn it around to your advantage. Meanwhile, you've created an alliance, which is the goal of any meeting.

～～～～

INTUITION IN ACTION
TENTACLING THE CLOCK

I was preparing for a meeting with Macary, a company with whom I (my company) wanted to create a strong alliance. My goal was to get the most profitable deal I could while still retaining control over the proposed joint venture. I wanted to know what would bring us to a resolution on the deal.

So I placed my tentacles on Macary and my own company. To sense the progression of the deal, I placed myself (again, my company) at the center of the clock. Here is what I recorded before the meeting, followed by my evaluation:

ONE O'CLOCK: A woman wants to help but cannot carry through.

TWO O'CLOCK: A storm creating a stalemate. Interpreted by the other side as an intentional stalemate.

THREE O'CLOCK: January. More information revealed that clarifies for both sides.

FOUR O'CLOCK: A stack of papers that I see in front of me. They contain good information, but they will never be read.

FIVE O'CLOCK: March. Chickens pecking at one another looking for where the food is.

SIX O'CLOCK: Okay. Everyone is ready to get to work. This needs to be resolved. Differences have cooled. Joint venture possible.

SEVEN O'CLOCK: One last grandstand of difficulties. I see us resisting engagement, giving them time to chase their own tail.

EIGHT O'CLOCK: The blue of a lake. The first reunion of positions and potentials. May; early May.

NINE O'CLOCK: Macary has difficulty. We have to address their weakness to strengthen the collaboration. We have the resources to do this at this time.

TEN O'CLOCK: Macary introduces us to some of their resources, which we want direct access to. North.

ELEVEN O'CLOCK: I see distance between us and Macary. They decide to focus on another geographical region. It supports our union. They find a partner who is disposed to strengthen our partnership with Macary. A foreign feeling.

TWELVE O'CLOCK: Six years from now. Our working alliance has dissolved peacefully, but our company has been strengthened by this affiliation. We now face the challenge of once again changing our structure.

〰〰〰

THE EVALUATION

From one o'clock to three o'clock seems to be what has happened in the past few months, but from a perspective I had not been aware of.

There are, I'm embarrassed to say, no women in our company who are working on this deal. Macary, however, has a female senior executive strongly opposed to the deal. It seems there's been some confusion, which has been interpreted negatively.

In January a consultant came in to help us generate some solutions, but I wasn't sure he had been effective. To be honest, I haven't really reviewed the notes. I think four o'clock is telling me that I should.

Five o'clock tells me that I should have a brainstorming session to clarify what our needs and expectations are and what theirs are. Maybe I will go over the consultant's notes first.

I take seven o'clock as a warning to keep a clear perspective on disagreements. I may do some more work on figuring out what these disagreements are about. Early May is a little later than I had hoped, but I think that we can do some revising to accommodate the delay. Maybe I should ask some questions about how to speed things up, but the rest of the reading is so positive for us that maybe the delay is useful to us.

The rest of the reading I will have to do some work on to verify the information. I feel more strongly than ever about persevering in these negotiations.

∼16∼

INTEGRATING INTUITION INTO
YOUR DECISION-MAKING PROCESS

FINDING THE LOST WALLET: AN ILLUSTRATION WITH A MORAL

A friend recently called me up, beside himself because he could not find his wallet. He was fairly sure it wasn't lost and hadn't been stolen. But after numerous exhaustive searches of his office and apartment, he was beside himself.

"I'm sure it will turn up in time," I said.

"I know, but it just bugs me that I can't find it. It's really driving me to distraction. Besides, I need to use my credit cards and driver's license. If I don't find my wallet soon, I'll have to report the cards stolen and waste a morning at the Motor Vehicle Bureau getting another license."

"Where do you remember last putting it?" I volunteered.

"I've gone through this a million times already," he said, not hiding his exasperation. "I've checked all the logical places. I can't find my wallet because it's obviously not in a logical place! I thought maybe you could help me with your intuition. You know, maybe give me some clues."

"Okay, but before I help you, I want you to help yourself," I said, since I had been training him in how to use his intuition. "Let's both, right now, get an intuitive fix on the wallet and when I count to three, we'll both say where it is."

"Okay," he said.

"One . . . two . . . three! Quick! Right now! Where is your wallet?!"

145

"On the floor!" he blurted out.

"That's what I got," I said, smiling. "Quickly now, office or apartment?!"

"My apartment!"

"That's my sense, too," I said.

"But that doesn't make any sense. What would my wallet be doing on the floor?"

"Remember," I said, "you're the one who said that you can't find the wallet because it's not in any logical place."

"You're right," he said, laughing. "Okay, I'm going to search every inch of my apartment. Thanks, Laura!"

"You're welcome," I said, and returned to playing with my young son.

Several hours later he called back.

"I can't believe this! I've searched every square inch of my apartment. I've checked under couches and in every cranny. Heck, I even checked behind the refrigerator, though my wallet would have had to fly out of my pocket to land there. I really don't know what to do, I was so sure."

Frankly, I was surprised, since I was fairly sure of my intuitive "hit," too. "Excuse me," I said, "I'll ask my son."

"Your son?"

"He's as intuitive as you or I am, and he's less likely to try to 'figure out' where the wallet is."

So I put the phone down and went to my son's playroom. "Honey, where is the missing wallet?"

Without looking up from his superhero figurines, he said, "It's on the floor." Mind you, he had heard none of the previous phone conversations. "Thank you," I said, and returned to the phone.

"He says it's on the floor."

"Well, that's really amazing. Three out of three. But I've already ransacked my apartment from top to bottom on my hands and knees. It's not on the floor."

"I don't know what else to say," I said.

"I'm sorry. It's not your fault," he said. "Thanks for your help. I'll just have to deal with it."

The next evening he called back, very excited. "You're not going to believe this!"

"What?" I asked.

"I found my wallet!"

"Congratulations!" I said. "Where was it? I'm curious."

"That's the funny thing. I couldn't shake the sense that it was on the floor, so in my desperation I decided to give the entire apartment one last search. And as I crawled around my living room, I moved my briefcase out of my way. It had fallen over, so I righted it. As I did so, I absentmindedly stuck my hand in a side pocket I never use—and there was my wallet! Isn't that funny? It was on the floor. My wallet was in the side pocket of my briefcase—lying on the floor! And I thought my briefcase was in my way!"

Discussion

Although this anecdote is not directly about business, it perfectly illustrates the strengths and limitations of both intuition and analysis (he began by searching all the logical places) and the importance of integrating both processes.

Never Make a Decision Based Solely on Intuition

Intuitive impressions alone do not provide enough information to make a fully informed decision. But then, neither does logic or emotion. To make your best decisions, you must use all three together. More precisely, you must *consciously* use all three together since you already do so unconsciously—often at cross-purposes.

This is an important point that intuition's skeptics conveniently overlook. Intuition should not and cannot be used in isolation. Intuition *supplements* hard thinking, it doesn't replace it! Those who deny intuition cut themselves off from an incredibly useful source of information that would not otherwise be available to them.

So let's agree that only by combining our intuition, logic, and emotions can we operate at our most effective levels. The important thing we will consider in this chapter is *how* they should be used together.

The Relative Role of Intuition and Analysis Will Vary

How you combine intuition and analysis will vary widely with the particular situation: whether you are buying a car, making an investment, choosing a career path, or dealing with a potential client. Here is a list of some situations when the conscious exercise of intuition comes in handy:

- **When information is sketchy or unreliable.** Is your information sufficient? Is it conflicting? Is it timely? Is it suspect? Intuition can come in handy in situations where you don't have all the facts, such as during negotiations—or finding lost wallets.
- **To anticipate the future.** The farther into the future you are trying to see, the less reliable your information or projections will be. The preeminent strength of intuition, of course, is in prediction.
- **As a check on logic.** People are just as likely to make a mistake in their rational thought processes as they are in using their intuition. Unfortunately, if there's a flaw in our reasoning or our assumptions, we often don't find out until it's too late. Intuition is especially attuned to subtle dangers like these that are otherwise so easy to overlook.
- **To get the "big picture."** Analysis is obviously useful in breaking complex situations down to manageable parts, but the result is that we often lose sight of the forest for the trees. Intuition looks for connections between parts and takes in the whole—which is again the integrity theme we've been exploring.
- **When I-mode is necessary.** Logic is not especially effective at perceiving the needs, beliefs, or values of individuals or corporations. Intuition, on the other hand, is tailor-made for situations involving integrity.
- **When time is of the essence.** Another great advantage of intuition over logical reasoning is speed. You rarely have enough time to make an exhaustive analysis of all your options. You can always take shortcuts in your analysis by making assumptions or using approximations, but that diminishes the reliability of your conclusions.
- **To suggest the most promising areas to investigate logically when you have too much information or too many options.** In the information age, we are overwhelmed by facts and often don't know where to begin. Intuition can help cut through the confusion and point you in the right direction.

This is an excellent example of the partnership possible between intuition and analysis. Scientists often begin their analysis with a hunch, which is then subjected to exhaustive scrutiny by their logical minds. Einstein, for example, claimed that his great ideas occurred to him first intuitively, but that afterward he had to verify them logically.

Another example is master chess players who use intuition to narrow their search from thousands of potential move variations down to a promising few that are then calculated precisely.

In the financial world, George Soros uses his intuition to warn him about his investments or to alert him to opportunities—but he doesn't bet billions solely on his hunches!

Again, this is a partial list of the role intuition can play in information-gathering and decision-making. Intuition can also be used in other areas like problem-solving or in the creative process.

DAILY PRACTICE
FINDING THE SILVER LINING

It's one thing to understand "in your head" that apparently negative outcomes may in fact be blessings in disguise, but it's another to realize this deep down in your heart and soul, in your unconscious. So from time to time conjure up situations that at first glance might seem undesirable for someone—or yourself!—and practice both your ability to deal with them and to recognize their hidden positive potential.

EXERCISE 22
DO YOU BALANCE YOUR LOGICAL AND
INTUITIVE PROCESSES?

The following quiz will help you gauge whether you effectively balance your intuition and logic in everyday life. This isn't a contest, so reply honestly below.

1. Do you know when or under what conditions you get your best ideas?

A. Yes, you've even developed "rituals" to cultivate the creative process. (4)

B. There seems to be a pattern, but you aren't sure. (2)

C. Your best ideas come completely randomly, so you couldn't really say. (0)

2. Out of the blue you get the idea to move to Paris. You are not involved in any significant relationship at this time, but it would involve giving up your job.

A. You give your employer two weeks' notice, put your belongings in storage, and book your flight. (2)

B. You reject the idea completely, especially since you can barely speak the language. (0)

C. You begin to investigate how you feel about such a move, and whether it would be practical. (4)

3. How often do you notice what's going on in your environment, both internal and external?

A. Often, if not on a daily basis. (4)

B. Often, though not regularly, and not in any formal way. (2)

C. Rarely, if ever. (0)

4. Have you ever been in a conversation with a new acquaintance or in a new situation and found yourself blurting out things that proved to be accurate?

A. No, never. (0)

B. You can remember a few specific instances in the last few years. (2)

C. So often that you're no longer even surprised by it. (4)

5. How do your hunches present themselves?

A. In random ways; there doesn't seem to be a pattern. (2)

B. In very specific ways. (4)

C. You can't say for sure. (0)

6. Your broker calls you up "to let you in on" a hot stock. Indeed, after reviewing the available research on the company, you are quite impressed with its prospects. In the back of your head, however, is a nagging feeling that something is not quite right.

A. You buy the stock aggressively on margin. (0)

> B. You use limited risk capital to purchase the stock or
> options on it. (4)
> C. You avoid the stock completely. (2)
> 7. Do you keep a regular journal?
> Λ. No. (0)
> B. Yes. (4)

20 to 28 points: Your intuitive, logical, and emotional processes are well-balanced. With some training, you could learn to gain even more conscious control over your intuition.

10 to 18 points: You are aware of your intuition, though it appears sporadically and is out of balance with your logical and emotional processes. Remember that intuition is just one component of decision-making, though an important one.

0 to 8 points: You are either unaware of your intuition, or you suppress it. You may also be denying certain emotional processes, as well. You need to open up more to nonrational modes of relating to the world.

~~17~~

HOW CAN I GET
OTHERS TO HELP ME?
(YOU HAVE TO UNDERSTAND AND
SATISFY THEIR NEEDS, TOO)

YOUR SUCCESS DEPENDS ON YOUR TEAM

You cannot succeed in business without a team behind you to help get what you have to offer to the market. But your team can also help you in another important way: by keeping you in touch with your market.

So far we have been addressing such situations as the person looking for work, or for a better job, or the entrepreneur or manager running a company. We have discussed the fact that maintaining integrity is paramount to the success of any individual or company. But until now we have been discussing ways in which you can use your intuition to maintain and enhance your integrity's balance point.

You are not without resources. No matter how intuitive you are, no matter how well you maintain your integrity's balance point, each member of your team can also help you stay in tune with and respond to the needs of your market and environment—not to mention the needs of the other team members.

To create flow, and from that the ability to move forward, the integrity of the company needs to be addressed. Each and every person or company on your team is receiving and interpreting information about you all of the time. I am continually amazed at how often the receptionist is more "product aware" than is the CEO. The evening clean-up staff or even your suppliers may have a better sense of who within your firm is underperforming.

Your team can best help you assess this if each member—like you—looks at the whole. Each member performs a different role, of course, so it is unlikely that they will have the same sense of the whole that you do.

But do not discount anyone's input. It may even be your young daughter who intuitively gets the sense that the market is heading down and can back her hunch up with information that makes sense to you.

Some companies are even going so far as to reveal sensitive internal financial documents not only to their employees but even to their suppliers. Any training programs your company offers should work to enhance the participants' awareness of the needs of everyone in your business world.

What Are You Offering the Members of Your Team?

Of course, your members may keep their best ideas for themselves if they no longer sense that a stronger company means better futures for them. Remember that the important thing they need to be aware of is not the overall integrity of your company or even how it is adding value to your market—but rather, how their best efforts for you will add value to them.

One way to see how you can add value to your team members is to look for the area in which people have focused their attention. Is it the internal running of the company, or the external market? Are many people in your company having personal difficulties? Are there personality conflicts within the company? Companies offering child care at work are on the right track because they create in the worker an investment in the workplace that moves beyond a job.

If one of the most overlooked sources of information is the people within your own company—and this may be true even if you have a "suggestion box"—you must find ways to establish communication lines with them. Meetings are a good place to start.

Using Meetings to Build Your Team's Integrity

Leading a meeting effectively is surely one of the hardest tasks in corporate life. You are surrounded by people who may not want to be there and who may not have their full attention on the subject at hand. Add to that the hidden agendas lurking in the heads of everyone at the table.

How is it ever possible to make this a productive use of both your time and theirs? My secret is to poll all the agendas at the meeting. Not only does this yank all the agendas out of hiding, but people can't keep themselves from participating—and enjoying it.

When a group of people work together toward the same goal (or in the same company), it is essential to create more connection than is created in the annual company picnic because more profound contact creates ideas and ideas motivate action. No success is static. To maintain success, the form of your company will change continually. Without integrity, which presupposes communication between the parts, a structure is hampered in its ability to respond effectively and thereby change productively.

A group meeting should include each person's insights beyond the scope of his or her "job." (The kitchen staff thinks that shipping is having difficulties because the new computer system is not working. And maybe, they add, it would be better to stick with the old system until the bugs are worked out.) People should be encouraged for their detailed observations—but don't put anyone on the spot about why they think something. If you want people to generate intuitive information, you don't want them to think too much about what they are saying (or be "put on the spot" in any way), and you want to commend them for their generosity in participating.

Employees (or other members of your team) should be seated next to those with whom they are least familiar (so that "clique formation" is avoided), and this should be rotated (cliques form quickly). Everyone should be urged to use "nondefensive language." Instead of saying something like, "Janet isn't communicating her needs to us and then complains when we can't fill those needs on time," a better line would be, "We would be able to better serve you, Janet, if you gave us three days' notice for any changes you need from us."

You can teach people to do this by setting an example yourself. When necessary, you can step in to rephrase a comment more constructively (or pick one of your employees with a talent in this area). You can simply say to your employees, "Think of a cooperative way to state your needs." The side benefit of asking people to do this openly is that initially there are a lot of laughs as people struggle to find inclusive (rather than battle flag) language when what they really want to say is, "The marketing department sucks!"

Consider asking people to drop their gripes in a box ahead of time (as well as their compliments) and tell them that they will be addressed at the appropriate time so that their personal agendas do not interfere with the flow of the meeting. You can also start the meeting with an area of general agreement or a low-conflict problem.

This method of communication works in a meeting of two people, a negotiation with a supplier, a job interview, or a conference of hundreds. It is inclusive and maintains the integrity of the group as well as creating integrity and communication when there is none.

THE TRICK TO ELICITING INTUITIVE RESPONSES

The purpose of some meetings, of course, is to communicate information or to analyze a situation. There will often be times, however, when you will want to solicit the intuitive impressions of your team members. To do this you must frame questions in such a way that the group needs to be inventive to answer them completely. Make sure that your questions have as little information as possible for the reasoning mind without making your team think you've gone mad.

Good opening lines for this sort of exercise are, "Let's bat around some ideas," or "Let's go wild," or "Let's throw things out on the table and see what comes up." One of the most helpful things you can say in a brainstorming meeting is that you want people to make mistakes! That's right. Explain that if someone is right all the time, you realize that they aren't giving everything they can give: "If fifty percent of what you say is not totally off the wall, then I know you all aren't trying." That really puts people in the position of having to toss out their ideas. In fact, I would tape these sessions because they are full of gems.

During these meetings, notice who on your team is coming up with good intuitive "hits" and who is more effective logically. Your goal is to create meetings where everybody has something to say about every other department, because people are generally inhibited when speaking about things outside their area of expertise.

One of the worst things about business today is that everyone is conserving his or her ideas. We've practically entered an era of idea conservation, because ideas are worth so much money. And ideas are one of the most valuable contributions your team members can give.

You might start by asking a question about your biggest competitor, a subject with which the group will be somewhat familiar—but ask an off-point question. If this is a meeting of the marketing division, ask a financial question: "How do you think their stock price will do this week?"

Even if your team doesn't follow the stock price, you'd be surprised, if you keep at it, by how many people will answer "off the top of their head." Coming from a family of doctors, I have seen many a good internist ask a patient, "What do you think is going on with your body?" and get the right answer. For that matter, I've asked strangers on the subway if the price of corn futures will go up today and have gotten correct responses.

Deliberately jump from topic to topic and then return to the topics at random. This short-circuits the reasoning process and promotes both intuitive and honest responses.

Here are some other examples:

- You're filling a new position but you don't think it would be appropriate for the group to interview the candidate. Give the group a few noncommittal details about the prospective employee that are unlikely to cause a reaction. "He was born in 1960 and received his B.A. from Stanford. I don't know, you saw him in the hallway, what impressions did you get from him? How do you feel he would be with the clients? I know you only saw him for a minute, but you are so accurate with your first impressions. Everyone feel free to jump in."

- You've convened a meeting to brainstorm new product ideas for a company like Procter & Gamble or Gillette. "If people in the music business had this challenge, what would they do?" you might ask. "How about the airline industry? The used-car business? The shoe business?" Obviously, here you want to get as far afield from personal products as possible to encourage "off-the-top-of-my-head" responses from everyone.

- Your company is in the last round of competition for a new account. Your presentation contains terrific ideas, but the format will be the same as everyone else's: graphs or slides. You'd like to do something different but realize that's risky. "You know, we've got the MacGregor presentation coming up next week," you might begin. "What do you think everyone else's presentation will look like?"

In the last example, the odds are that your team will be so focused on the content of your competitions' presentations that they'll have no clue about the format, so they'll be forced to answer spontaneously. Keep pushing if you get an "I don't know" answer. "Well, if you were our competitors, what would you do?"

Then quickly cut to a different subject altogether. "Say, I just saw that great movie last night. Oh, shoot, what was the name of it?" People will chime in with the names of several current films. Verify that one of them was the one you saw, but then ask what they liked about all the others.

A friend of mine did this once with an advertising agency client. The client's company was in a tight race with more established firms to land a banking account. The team members ended up comparing the movies *Dumb and Dumber* and *Animal House*, which in turn reminded the client of his college fraternity days, which then reminded him of the variety shows he had emceed in college, which then made him think of skits, and which finally made him slap the table and yell, "We won't draw the storyboards, we'll act them out!"

He did, and his agency won the account.

ADDING TO YOUR TEAM

Hiring is a real weak spot for any company, large or small. Let's say that you or your company are on a roll, and you want to keep it that way. How do you make sure you continue to hire the right people? I think there is a weak spot that comes even before that, which is that entrepreneurs and innovators tend to make poor managers.

So let's say you have a hot new company, and you finally hit that pinnacle. But your management team consists of the wild gorillas who launched the company. And now you don't need gorillas, you need suits. So you always need to look at your existing personnel first. And I think it makes for a better company—think integrity—to try to make personnel mobile, as opposed to letting them go. So you tell them honestly in the beginning that you are trying to conserve the jobs and the people in them.

And you tell them that you're going to suggest moves, but you refuse to suggest final solutions; that they have to do on their own. But that's step one.

Step two is to see your goal. Your goal should not be expressed in narrow terms like: "We need to hire five more people in each department" or "This department needs to do this, and that department needs to do that." You should first ask the broader question: What is needed right now? What does this department need to do right now?

Step three is to get your intuitive "hit," which may be different from what logic suggests. For example, you may have increased shipments so you are willing to increase staffing in that department but intuitively you may feel you need to downsize.

That doesn't make any sense to you when all of a sudden you realize, "Aha! We need to subcontract out our shipping system; it's too ineffective internally."

So first you have to ask the broad question and then allow yourself to see what is needed. You'll know your intuition was speaking if your gut impression went against what your analysis suggested.

This is one way to tell if your "hit" is valid. Most of the time, intuition won't tell you something your logic already knows with certainty. So if it's telling you something your logic already knows, you are not intuiting. And if your intuition is telling you nothing, then everything is probably going fine.

So you hire by holding in your mind some basic integrity questions—What does my company need, and who does it need?—and then you allow your intuition to find a fit.

REMEMBER TO CONSIDER THE WHOLE MIX

Sometimes you need to look on the personal level, on the departmental level, and on the level of the whole organization. You may have the perfect person on one level, but once you put him into the mix, the overall impact is to reduce your company's effectiveness.

If that's the case, the next question is, Who needs to be let go? And if someone needs to be let go, why not let that person go now? Your preference, as we discussed earlier, should be to transfer the person to another department, sooner rather than later.

~~~~~

AN INTUITIVE TALE

My most recent experience with intuition in business occurred four months ago. It came to me that I should create a new vendor file in a format that not only gave names and addresses, but that also cross-referenced the products or services they provided, just in case our packaging director left the company.

I asked my assistant, who was the resident computer maven, to assist the packaging director in the project so that it didn't pull her away from her daily responsibilities. Several months later, the packaging director sent me E-mail requesting vacation time. I suggested that she come in to talk to me about it because I had the sense that she was leaving the company. When I asked her, she said no and that she was very happy.

Less than a month later she came in to speak to me, shaking nervously. She came in to resign because she had accepted a job, which represented a significant promotion, at a leading international cosmetics company.

~~~~~

~18~

THE INTUITIVE PROCESS
AS A SYSTEM

USING YOUR INTUITION EFFECTIVELY REQUIRES A SYSTEMATIC PROCESS

My training as a teenager was all in math and science, which, ironically, taught me that the intuitive process is as rigorously logical and disciplined as the scientific method. As you've discovered, there is a lot more to using your intuition than simply "blurting out the first thing that comes to mind" and "going with your gut."

Here's a sampling of everything you must keep track of:

- Realizing what, specifically, you're "observing" and the precise question you're considering.
- Noticing all your impressions without unconsciously excluding or editing anything.
- Keeping your intuitive impressions distinct from your thoughts and feelings.
- Searching and probing for deeper and richer connections.
- Interpreting the relevance of these impressions.
- Verifying your conclusions.
- Integrating your intuitive impressions with your logical and emotional ones.

Yet, with practice, this will be a completely natural and even automatic process, if it isn't already.

DEVELOPING YOUR INTUITION MAY IMPROVE YOUR THINKING!

When was the last time you subjected your everyday thinking to this kind of scrutiny? What's clear, in fact, is that the effective use of our intuition may require even more precision and disciplined awareness than we apply to our "logical" thinking, which most of the time is on automatic pilot, if not downright sloppy. You may find that a secondary benefit to developing your intuitive reasoning is that you'll become more aware of your logical reasoning process and its own peculiarities and pitfalls.

DEVELOPING A STEP-BY-STEP METHOD

Your intuition will, of course, continue to operate without your conscious control, but when you want to apply it to answer a specific question, here are the steps:

STEP ONE: Begin with a body check as a baseline check before you begin your reading.

STEP TWO: Direct your intuitive attention with a carefully framed question.

STEP THREE: Report what you notice in response to the question.

STEP FOUR: Interpret these impressions.

STEP FIVE: Elaborate them to create verifiable scenarios.

STEP SIX: Verify your conclusions.

STEP SEVEN: Weigh them, along with your thoughts and emotions.

Again, you don't need to memorize these steps. The actual process is more seamless, and with experience you can mold it to your personal style. With practice, this conscious process will become a habit, a frame of mind you "slip into" as easily and naturally as you do when you reason. At that point, your intuition, an unconscious and haphazard process made conscious and disciplined, will once again become unconscious!

DEVELOPING INTUITION AS A HABIT

As you have more experience of your own intuitive process, you'll be able to tailor your own system, which will more effectively match your unique style, needs, and situation. Part of that, of course, is getting in touch with how intuition works for you.

Two habits in particular will help you develop access to your intuition on demand: turning everything into questions and practicing quick hits.

YOU CAN TURN ANYONE OR ANYTHING INTO A QUESTION

Intuition functions to bring us useful information in response to questions. The more you make the questioning process conscious, the more control you'll gain over your intuition.

You're reading the morning paper and see someone's name in the first article. What does this person need? If you were a company, how would you market your product or service to him?

Your boss has turned to you for new product ideas to serve existing markets. What does your market most value that you have to offer? How can you present your product in a way this market perceives as addressing its needs?

By turning everything into a question—especially the I-mode questions—you get a continuous stream of answers. That is the intuitive "position of attention."

CONTINUALLY INVENT QUICK-HIT EXERCISES

Quick-hit exercises are a great way to get immediate feedback on your intuitive process. When you've finished the last chapter of this book, continue to invent your own versions. They're fun and a great way to spend idle time. With practice, you'll be able to devise ones tailored to your specific profession. A salesperson might target potential customers, while a stockbroker or an investor might target the stock market.

In chapter 22, in fact, we'll be putting all our techniques together to predict the stock market.

～～～

INTUITION IN ACTION
Robert Earl, Founder of Planet Hollywood

I differed with Laura in that I thought my ability to see a complex business situation—either a problem or an opportunity—was based on informed knowledge rather than pure intuition.

If I had seen two years ago, as I did, that London would be the hottest city in the world, it was based on my travels, on my seeing a whole new young breed of artists and musicians; it was based on my knowledge of history and cycles; it was based on all the indicators of where international companies need to be in the next twenty years and why they all had to come back to London.

For example, when I solve a problem, I don't do it in isolation. I fight on every level at the same time. That's where most businesspeople might go wrong. I can't clean up one problem, then move on to the next. Anything can go wrong. I like to have all the balls in the air at the same time. So I fight on multiple fronts. That is my approach to life. I cover every aspect, or at least I attempt to.

The first thing I always do is get the big picture. I'm a real macro thinker. When I'm confronted with a crisis situation, I educate myself about every aspect: financial, organizational, marketing, and so on. I get the big picture first, then I do an enormous amount of diligent work and immerse myself in the details. I'm definitely a planner. I write everything down.

Now that I think about it, though, I must use my intuition because I'm always taking on completely new situations and somehow I know instantly what to do.

～～～

DISCUSSION

Robert Earl is an incredibly smart, enormously successful entrepreneur. He has gotten where he is through a combination of talent and experience and hard work. But the world is filled with talented, hard-working individuals, many of whom have seen the same things that Robert Earl has seen. Yet somehow Earl has been able to put all the puzzle pieces together and create a plan of action that built an entertainment empire.

~19~

HOW CAN I PREVENT OTHERS
FROM INTERFERING?
(AGAIN, YOU MUST CONSIDER THEIR NEEDS)

WHO—OR WHAT—IS YOUR ENEMY?

We tend to look at enemies as "the bad guys" or the ones "out to get us." In the business world, we see our enemies as "the competition."

But intuition and integrity offer us a larger, more fundamental—and ultimately more useful—view of the enemy: anyone or anything working toward goals that conflict with yours, or in ways that prevent you from achieving yours. (On the flip side, of course, your allies are anyone or anything working toward the same goals as you, or in ways that help you achieve yours.)

- Sometimes your enemies are obvious, as in another person suddenly competing for the same promotion that had been promised to you.
- Sometimes your enemies are not so obvious, especially when their hidden agenda is at odds with your goals.
- And sometimes *you* are the enemy, when your hidden agenda is at odds with your own goals. This is what we mean when we use the phrase "He is his own worst enemy."

Note also that your enemy need not be someone you know; it need not even be a person. If you own stocks and your congressional representative proposes to increase the capital gains tax, your representative and even the bill he or she is sponsoring are your enemies.

Finally, note that the same person or company can be your enemy regarding one goal, but your ally regarding another. Successful corporations realize this when they form alliances with a company in one market while competing in another.

STAY FOCUSED ON INTEGRITY—YOUR OWN AND OTHERS

We are taught to think that safety comes from external vigilance of things that influence our business, like our market or our competitors. This is a mistake.

By using your intuition instead to maintain the focus on your company's integrity and the integrity of those within it, you achieve the same results. You are still tuned in to your environment but you are also directing your attention—and power—toward the organization. This allows you to respond flexibly to your environment and challenges rather than disperses your attention and energy outward toward the many elements that are largely beyond your control (although now within your foresight and ability to respond to intuitively).

NOBODY MANAGED PROPERLY IS AN ENEMY

It is a rare situation when someone wants to harm you or your company simply for the sake of doing harm. Usually, it is a simple competition for resources that often can be addressed creatively so that the win-lose situation becomes a win-win one.

How do you achieve this? By changing your enemy's perspective and demonstrating that the perceived conflict can be resolved by aligning his or her agenda with yours. There are always ways to present your goals in a favorable light—remember: No one can help you with a goal if they are unaware of it—and to expose someone else's agenda in a cooperative way (tell your coworker how much you appreciate her cooperation in validating management's decision to promote you and suggest that in you she will have an ally for the next promotion that comes along).

Not only do you appear pleasant, you have alerted her to the fact that you are on to her game and won't let it jeopardize you. What's more, you have helped divert her energy into a mutually beneficial alliance and outcome.

Forewarned is forearmed. And since reframing a problem allows your enemy to see the goals you have in common, the person is now an ally.

THE IMPORTANCE OF FRAMING

The situation above is an example of "reframing" a problem or conflict, a powerfully effective way to handle enemies by creating agreement.

Since most goals require the cooperation of others, you have to find a way to describe yours so that everyone involved sees the value in reaching it. You must "frame" your goal—that is, make it compelling enough that others will want to help you accomplish it.

Again, this is maintaining the integrity of your business world. By training yourself always to consider the needs and values of everyone in your business world, you are better able to find productive frameworks.

The framework you must use will vary from person to person. If your goal is to start a company, the framework you use with a banker or an investor will differ from the one you use with an employee or a supplier.

The following example will show you how to apply framing in your own life. This situation was actually a hypothetical scenario presented to me by Hearst New Media in a live Internet interview, followed by my response.

～～～～～

INTUITION IN ACTION
HE STOLE MY IDEA!

I know it was my idea, because I got it after fighting with my boyfriend.

Dave was yelling that I spend too much time at *Smooch,* where I sell ads. "*Smooch* is a ridiculous name for a magazine," he said. "It won't last." He thinks print media is dead and people only read on the Web now.

Even worse, he said that *Smooch's* target audience is supposed to be twenty-somethings, but everyone knows that only teenagers read the magazine.

On the subway I fantasized about dumping him, but suddenly his words flashed through my head: "Thirteen-year-olds read it. I've seen them." What if he's right? Shouldn't we be selling ad pages to Clearasil instead of advertising mutual funds and Scotch?

I ran into Paul, the editor-in-chief, and suggested it. He said no, it would alienate some readers, since people in their twenties don't even want to think about ads for pimple cream. I decided not to pursue it.

Later, Amy, our publisher, told me that Paul wanted *Smooch* to start courting the teen market! Nice to know our editor-in-chief is such an original thinker.

I guess there's nothing I can do. Paul's not even in sales, he's just trying to look good. Paul and Amy seem close. He probably refined my idea and took the pimples out of it. But it was mine.

EXERCISE 23
REFRAMING AGENDAS

Pop Quiz: Use your intuition to suggest what Gail, *Smooch's* head of advertising sales, should do next. Which of the following options should she choose:

CHOICE 1: Lie low, say nothing, and be more confident—and discreet—about her next idea?

CHOICE 2: Confront Paul and tell him she feels betrayed?

CHOICE 3: Tell Amy that Paul presented her idea as his own?

Make your selection and then justify it in terms of everyone's goals and hidden agendas. Important: To get "full credit" for this exercise, you must also decide how Gail should frame her response. (Hint: Stay focused on the integrity of everyone's goals.)

DISCUSSION

First, Gail needs to illuminate her goal, which illustrates the power of reframing:

- Her goal: To reap the rewards from Dave's idea (not to expose Paul—see the difference already?).

Keeping this firmly in mind, she needs to let her intuition find Paul's goal and his hidden agenda:

- Paul's goal: To receive credit for having insight into the big picture.
- Paul's hidden agenda: To get closer to Amy.

She then needs to intuit Amy's goal and any hidden agenda she might have:

- Amy's goal: To make *Smooch* and herself as publisher a success.
- Amy's hidden agenda: To protect her closeness with Paul.

Choice 1 means not gaining anything from the idea while creating a situation in which she stifles her ability to be openly creative and work as a team. Better to find a new job.

Choice 2, on the other hand, could create more difficulty by putting Paul on the defensive. "Once burned, twice shy," as the old saying goes.

Choice 3 allows Gail to avoid confrontations altogether by using her intuition. Again, the important thing is how she tells Amy.

She should respond to both Amy's goal and her hidden agenda by telling her this: "I am so happy that Paul listened to what I had to say last week about courting the teen market. It is really great to have such a responsive editor-in-chief. But, to be frank, it was not my idea, it was my boyfriend's. So I talked with him further and then assembled some other data on this approach.

"Here is the marketing plan I have come up with. I would love to get Paul's opinion, since he initially felt that we would be alienating some of our readers. He makes a good point. I would like his opinion on how we can avoid doing that."

Taking this tack, everyone gets what he or she wants and avoids what he or she doesn't want. By pursuing this path, our Gail may end up with two allies rather than one ally and one enemy. Also note that

she maintained her integrity by giving proper credit to the real origina-
tor of the idea—her boyfriend, whom she was planning to dump!

SOMETIMES, UNFORTUNATELY, THE OTHER PERSON IS OUT TO GET YOU

We noted earlier that nobody is necessarily an enemy. In almost every
situation in which you find yourself, your intuition will reveal a way to
maintain the integrity of everyone's goals and agendas so that it's a win-
win situation. But what if Paul's hidden agenda in the example above
actually were to engage himself in battle?

In that case, Gail's question wouldn't be "How do I respond to this
issue?" but "How do I create odds against the battle of Paul?"

So her goal would change. But it would change in looking at the
question in terms of how she achieves her goal and makes the best out
of this idea for herself. How might Gail respond in that situation?

Her intuition might suggest speaking to Jennifer, head of public relations. Gail doesn't see how Jennifer can help, but she takes her to lunch.
Not to "talk about a problem" necessarily—unless her intuition suggested
this tack—but just to listen to Jennifer. At this point, of course, Gail's
intuition has pointed her in a direction, but now Gail needs more than
intuitive information.

And over the course of lunch Jennifer reveals that she moved over to
public relations because Paul "had it in for her, too" last year. This suggests other ideas to Gail, who might now choose to reveal her conflict
with Paul. And now she and Jennifer can combine their resources to
help Gail in this situation.

Gail might not have the final solution over lunch, but now she has
new questions on which she can focus her intuition.

~~~~~

DAILY PRACTICE
FRAMING YOUR ENEMIES' AND COMPETITORS' GOALS

From time to time, use I-mode to become your competitor or enemy. As you
do so, ask yourself the following questions:

- What would help you become larger and stronger?

• Is there any way to frame your goals or theirs to find agreement?

This may not always be possible, but you will surprise yourself with how often it is.

~~~~~~

REMEMBER: TURN EVERYONE AND EVERYTHING INTO A QUESTION

This example also illustrates the importance of a concept we discussed earlier. The key to reframing a contentious issue successfully is to ask the kind of questions for which you can generate solutions.

Even though our saleswoman Gail is angry at Paul, she does not act on the question, "How can I get revenge?" That would make everyone her enemy—a tactic which, over time, would cause her to lose her job. Instead, she aims to capitalize on the positive—creating a new advertising market—that might open up new career opportunities for herself.

Turning everyone and everything into constructive questions is an especially valuable tool for leaders of groups, whether you are leading a meeting or leading a company. Developing an intuitive dialogue allows you to address unspoken agendas productively.

In group settings, before acting, you should always try to figure out the situation by using your intuition to find hidden agendas. For example, Gail would not have wanted to confront Amy by announcing, "Paul stole my idea." They may be lovers for all she knows, and it wouldn't be hard to see where Amy's loyalties would lie.

So even if your intuition is not able to pick up exactly what's going on, it will give you a sense of where the links are—and where to tread lightly!

MAINTAIN YOUR PERSPECTIVES

The three "I's" when addressing an enemy are "I" the goal, "I" the environment, and "I" the arsenal.

"I" the goal is your conscious goal rather than your hidden agenda. Keep your focus on your goal rather than on your enemy or yourself. This keeps you at an objective distance and allows you to respond quickly to changes in your enemy's strategy or tactics.

"I" the environment includes your adversary but may also include people, elements, or changes in terrain of which you are not consciously aware when going into the situation.

"I" the arsenal are the allies, ideas, positions, phrases, mannerisms, or anything you do or could have at your disposal to address the situations that could arise.

Keep in mind that you'll need to approach the same three "I's" from your enemy's point of view. So when considering your environment—which includes your enemy—you must also consider the following:

- "I" the enemy's goal (and hidden agenda)
- "I" the environment from the enemy's perspective
- "I" the enemy's arsenal

Your ultimate goal, as I mentioned above, is to use your intuition to creatively resolve the various agendas that best promote your overall integrity.

Managing "Enemies" in the Business World

Andrew S. Grove, president and CEO of Intel Corporation, revealed his business thinking in the recently published book *Only the Paranoid Survive*. In it Grove wonders whether the widespread use of the Internet, especially the World Wide Web, is a "strategic inflection point" for Intel. These "SIPs," as he calls them, are moments of massive change when companies must alter direction quickly and drastically or risk annihilation—a potential enemy if ever there was one. The risk the Internet poses for Intel is that it could be accessed from a machine that does not contain an Intel microprocessor. The result would be a catastrophic loss of demand for Intel's primary product.

Grove, like most highly successful CEOs, uses his analytical mind to make a list of the pros and cons of the Internet for Intel. The positives slightly outnumber the negatives. He further reasons that so much "creative energy and funds are pouring in" to Internet development that new applications will be created for Intel's chips. Moreover, new players on the scene "are just as likely to play the role of allies as competitors," another piece of good news. Finally, he assesses his employees, concluding that they will not be overwhelmed by the Internet phenomenon.

Having considered the integrity of his business world, Grove said that his "gut" told him that the Internet was not a "grenade" threatening Intel's very existence. Of course, he could have reached this conclusion a great deal faster had he reversed the process—viewing Intel's situation with his intuition first and then later checking the evidence to support it (doing both before committing significant capital to any decisions).

In a remarkably candid display, he freely admits that "as the CEO, I could very well be the last one to notice" that a grenade had rolled in. Thus, while all the "classic signs" suggest that the Internet is not a strategic inflection point for Intel, "the totality of all the changes is so overwhelming that deep down I think it is," he writes.

Having allowed his intuition to win after all, Grove sets about changing his behavior to more properly manage this potential "enemy." Among other actions, he:

- Learns everything he can about the Internet and the World Wide Web through reading and "surfing."
- Visits other companies, "including those that at first blush might be regarded as the enemy because they are devoted to diminishing our business by putting an Internet appliance on the market as a substitute for PCs."
- Communicates the significance of the Internet to the entire company by adding a fourth objective to Intel's initial three, directing employees to mobilize their efforts in connection with the Internet.

But he leaves the most important change for the last paragraph of his book. Conceding again that he is "likely to be the last one to know" if a cheap Internet appliance will become popular, he decides to "build the best inexpensive Internet appliance that can be built, around an Intel microchip."

How's that for managing your enemies? If you can't beat 'em, join 'em—on your terms.

Grove utilized all three "I's" in analyzing and, it appears, neutralizing the potential threat the Internet posed for his company. By changing his perceptions, he was able to change his goals and behavior. In so doing, he also changed his company's goals and behavior, and in the process changed his marketplace. Given Grove's track record, would you want to bet against him?

AS GOALS AND SITUATIONS CHANGE, HOWEVER, SO DO YOUR ENEMIES

As a final note, remember that you must continually survey your various "I's" to monitor the effect of shifting goals and priorities. As your situation changes, or your goals, former allies can become enemies and former enemies can become allies.

~~~~~~

DAILY PRACTICE
HAVE YOU ACQUIRED ANY NEW ENEMIES?

In most situations, your intuition can "win over" enemies by finding frames within which to align everyone's goals. To do so, however, you must be aware of the ever-changing status of goals. Do any changes in your business world create new enemies for you—or new allies?

~~~~~~

~~~~~~

INTUITION IN ACTION
A LAWYER'S TALE

Shortly before the start of a trial in a divorce action involving a five-year, childless marriage between a couple in their mid-fifties, my client acquired an asset having a value of approximately $20 million. Under state law, the court had no power to give the wife a share of the value of this asset in the event of a divorce between the parties because the asset had been acquired by my client *after* he had commenced the divorce action against his wife.

To protect her financial interests, my client's wife decided to defend against the divorce. If she were to be successful in her defense, the divorce action would be dismissed. Then, she could bring a new action in which she would sue my client for divorce. Since this valuable asset would have been acquired *prior* to the commencement of the second divorce action, the court in that action would have the power to give the wife a share.

At the trial, which was before a six-member jury, my client testified that his wife had verbally and emotionally abused him and that her conduct, typically while she was under the influence of alcohol, met a legal standard for a divorce: She had treated him in a cruel and inhumane manner so as to render it unsafe or improper for him to live with her. Because virtually all of his wife's behavior occurred in the privacy of the home, my client had no witnesses to confirm his account as to his wife's behavior. Consequently, the jury would be likely to resolve the issue of my client's entitlement to a divorce on the basis of its evaluation of the respective credibility of my client and his wife.

After my client testified, his wife took the stand. She softly, but firmly, denied each allegation that my client had made against her. As she spoke, she made appropriate eye contact with the members of the jury. The cadence of her voice, together with the fluidity with which she delivered her account of the pertinent events, seemed to impress the jury and to persuade it as to her veracity.

As soon as the wife's denial of the last of the allegations had registered with the jury, the wife's attorney ended his examination of her by saying triumphantly, "No further questions." As the wife's attorney smugly walked back to his seat at the counsel table and as I rose to launch into the beginning of my cross-examination, which my client and I had carefully scripted on the preceding day, the wife glanced at the jury and announced gratuitously, "I was a wonderful wife."

Upon hearing the wife's ad-lib remark to the jury, I had an intuition. Although I had believed that the wife's denials were false, until her last statement I did not know whether the wife was purposefully telling falsehoods or whether she was "in denial," simply refusing to acknowledge her abusive behavior or the effect of her behavior upon my client. In an instant, I had the intuition that the cornerstone of her testimony was denial, not fabrication.

Immediately, I decided to do something far different from what my client and I had previously planned. Destruction of the wife's credibility from the outset of my cross-examination of her had been a prime goal. I saw a new way to achieve that goal. But with the jury waiting for me to ask the first question, I had no time to explain my intuition to my client. I simply asked my client for a vote of confidence: "Do you trust me?" He looked at me with panic written on his face. He realized that I was about to change the game plan, but he did not know what the new plan would be. He answered, unhappily and somewhat anxiously, "Yes."

I approached the wife and asked her a simple question in the warmest, kindest, most sympathetic, and most reassuring voice I could muster: "You never did anything wrong, did you?" The question took the wife by surprise; with a somewhat quizzical expression, she began to ponder it. At that moment, I realized that my intuition had been correct.

As the wife thought, I decided to give intuition an assist. I smiled warmly at the wife; I nodded my head ever so slightly up and down as if to say, "It's okay; we all know you were a wonderful, perfect wife; it might sound somewhat egotistical, but go ahead, you can say it—because it's true." The wife correctly read my message, and she seemed to be reassured by it. After a few seconds more had passed, she began to nod her head ever so slightly up and down in agreement and said, "You're right, I never did anything wrong."

The jury returned a verdict in favor of my client. After the judge dismissed the jury, several jury members told me that the case had been slightly against my client until the wife gave the answer to the question that my intuition inspired me to ask. They said that anyone who believed she had never done anything wrong was not credible. Accordingly, the jury declined to believe the wife's denials of the allegations against her, largely on the basis of the wife's answer to my intuitive question.

Thanks to my intuition and my trust in it, my client won the trial. That night, we celebrated at La Côte Basque, a four-star restaurant. While savoring the bouquet of a first-growth Bordeaux, my client smiled and said, "Thank you. If it weren't for your intuition, we would probably be dining in my new room at Payne-Whitney"—a psychiatric hospital.

<hr />

~~20~~

KNOWING HOW TO
ACT ON YOUR INTUITION

HOW MUCH CAN YOU RELY ON YOUR INTUITION?

You're now at the point in your intuitive training when you have developed it into a fairly reliable tool for gaining information useful in answering your questions. Intuition has the ability to give us facts—from the past, present, and future—about the things we need to know. Once you have that information, how do you know how to *act* on it?

A stockbroker recently told me, "I can make three million dollars in a month by following my hunches, but sometimes they don't work." I asked him to give me an example of when his "hunches" didn't work. He said that he recently had a strong visual impression of his positions literally slipping off a hill—and a few days later they did, costing him a great deal of money.

I suggested that his intuition was working for him, but he wasn't working with it; an intuitive message isn't worth much if you don't heed it! Here is the ideal process for verifying an intuitive impression:

- Record as many of your hunches as you can.
- Record your judgments, hopes, and fears as well as anything in your personal life that could be influencing the way you feel.
- Search all the available information to see if your hunches are substantiated by anything else in the environment (a profit

announcement due from the company, the threat of political upheaval, and so on).
- With all this information in hand, make a reasoned decision that includes your intuitive data and an awareness of your biases in that moment.

YOU DON'T HAVE TO TRUST YOUR INTUITION!

Coming from an intuitive, this statement always surprises people. You'll often hear advice like "trust your gut" or "go with your instincts" or "follow your hunches." To me these phrases are as silly as saying "trust your logic" or "go with your emotions."

The problem with "trust your gut" is that this advice assumes that the only thing you have to go on is faith.

That is completely wrong. The whole point to the intuitive process is that you create verifiable markers that you can then verify through logical analysis or the available evidence.

People don't believe in their own intuition until they experience it. Nor should they. I am a firm believer in calling belief just that, and keeping it in the "file" where you keep belief or faith. Fact is fact and belief is belief. Intuition uncovers *facts*.

In the rare cases when a hunch cannot be immediately verified—as in the case of a future event—you can usually use other checks and balances, such as time lines, to create advance warning signals that you may have misinterpreted your intuitive impressions. The only time you should rely solely on intuition is when you have no other choice.

So if you are a skeptic who doesn't "believe in" intuition—good for you! Belief has no place in arenas where proof is available. My five-year-old son didn't believe he could master Nintendo either, even while he was mastering it. He had all the skills necessary to play the game; he simply had never organized and focused them.

Similarly, you don't have to believe in intuition for it to work for you. In the end, the only way to "prove" that intuition works is for people to experience how accurate their own intuition can be and how much useful information it can provide. Simply do the exercises, follow the directions, and suspend judgment long enough to let your intuition prove its usefulness. It will!

A PERSONAL CONFESSION

Having said all that, I must admit that I buy real estate on intuition alone. A decade ago I had recently gotten back from Italy, and had decided to walk down to Tribeca, at that time a rather desolate neighborhood in New York City, to view some loft apartments for sale. I fell in love with a large unit and two smaller ones so I asked the building owner their asking prices.

Right there I decided to go with the two smaller units and countered with a bid one-third less than the asking price, with the further stipulation that my offer would expire in twenty-four hours. In the ten years since the owner accepted my offer, Tribeca has become one of the city's hottest neighborhoods and my apartment's value has appreciated over 500 percent.

I found my apartment in Rome in pretty much the same way. I found myself one day in a ghetto neighborhood, fell in love with a tiny apartment, and bought it strictly on instinct. I didn't do any research at all—and then watched the neighborhood gentrify around me.

I was fortunate with both investments since I am skilled at using my gut instinct to make decisions. On the other hand, I've learned the importance of backing up my hunches. I didn't realize it at the time, but the building owner accepted my low bids on his lofts because they were the last two he needed to qualify for the building's certificate of occupancy. I doubt I could have discovered that information through research, nor would I even have known to investigate such matters.

Still, I knew intuitively that the seller was anxious to sell not one but two apartments. If I had made my offer on the larger unit instead, I would not have solved the building owner's time problem. My gut told me that the price break was on the smaller units, so I went with my hunch, which has since proved to have been a wise decision.

YOU ALWAYS HAVE SAFEGUARDS

Let's say you're in a situation calling for action or an immediate decision when you aren't able or don't have the time to verify your intuition, which is sending you a strong signal. Here are some things to keep in mind:

- **If the situation involves real danger—act now, verify later!** If your intuition is warning you about something serious, get yourself out of danger immediately and then look for verification. For example, you wake up one morning and your intuition "screams" at you to sell your stock position in a certain company. By the time you have convinced yourself logically or empirically that this is a good idea, it may be too late. The company might announce bankruptcy and your stock would be worthless.

My recommendation would be to sell your stock (or hedge with "put" options) to be safe rather than sorry. If you were wrong, the worst thing that would happen is that you would miss out when the stock increased in value.

This advice is also true in situations that pose personal danger. If you're walking down the street at night and get a sense of a threat, then by all means do whatever you have to do to get yourself out of harm's way. Sometimes in these situations we're afraid of "looking foolish" or of "overreacting." This is certainly not a time to "wait for all the facts"—indeed, you hope that you're overreacting!

- **Try to buy yourself some time.** You're in an important negotiation and you're suddenly overwhelmed by the urge to leave the meeting. What do you do? Feeling awful about something isn't always a sign that it's a bad move, but there are ways in which your intuitive self let's your "self" know to stop, or go, or wait a while and look around.

  Do a quick body check to see if your instinct is good intuition or if you're just running scared. For example, do you feel unsafe? Or does walking out create an opportunity for you? Learn to distinguish what your body is telling you so that you don't destroy yourself in the moment. Can the action wait until a particular meeting is over?

  There's also another way to do this. Interrupt the meeting and say, "Hey, guys, it's a little dry in here. Why don't we take a break and get something to drink and then come back to the meeting? We can keep talking on the way." That way you get everyone out into the hall and solve your problem completely.

- **Test the waters.** Sometimes you don't need to make a complete commitment to a certain course of action. In our previous stock example, one alternative would be to sell, say, half your posi-

tion for some partial protection. The same is true of opportunities. Your instincts might be telling you to buy a stock but that
doesn't mean you have to mortgage your home and invest your
life savings.

- **If you have nothing to lose, go for it!** The key to using intuitive information is this: You often risk nothing by using it.
You're a real estate agent, so you ask your clients what they're
looking for and in what price range. The couple tells you
they're looking for something modern and that they "won't
spend more than $300,000." But your intuition tells you that
what they really want is something old-fashioned, with a white
picket fence, and that they would go up to $400,000 on just
such a property, which you have. You have nothing to lose by
driving them past the house on the way to something else
they've requested.

    Or let's say you're at a job interview and you get the sense
that the interviewer is a passionate fly fisherman, also one of
your interests. You have nothing to lose and everything to gain
by casually dropping in a reference to fishing and checking out
his response.

AGAIN: KNOW YOUR STRENGTHS AND LIMITATIONS

A big part of your intuitive training has been completing exercises that
give you immediate feedback about your intuitive process. We've made
a project out of your doing daily quick hits in a variety of situations. By
reviewing your journal notes, you should have a fairly good idea of
when your hunches are reliable and when they are less so.

I know for myself that most of my incorrect information comes to
me emotionally. If the impression comes with a strong emotion, it's usually not right even if it's out of the blue. If I feel panic, or fear, then I
know the data I'm getting isn't right.

Actually, for most people, emotion is the enemy of intuition because
the two are easily mistaken for each other. Emotion is an intricate bio-
chemical process that occurs in our glandular system, but it isn't intuition.

The most frequent example I hear in my workshops is, "I met this
woman and I knew she was perfect for me!" This is a hormonal

response, not necessarily an intuitive one. You're simply feeling alive. Or responding to body language. Or maybe the person looks like your mother or father.

But if I get a feeling, a body sensation, then the hunch is usually right. So if someone says, "I've got this great new job offer," and I feel my energy go out of me, I know it's not going to be good. If, however, it's a simple feeling, as opposed to an emotion, I know it's right.

You may be different. Some people are able to receive accurate intuitive information emotionally. You have to see what mechanism is right for you. My body and my physical senses, especially vision, are usually extremely accurate.

EXERCISE 24
GETTING IN TOUCH WITH YOUR INTUITIVE STYLE

Now that you are much more conscious of your intuition and have completed many exercises giving you feedback about it, it's a good time to become more aware of your intuitive process. Answering the following questions will help you recognize when you can safely rely on your intuitive impressions and when you should be more cautious.

- **Through which sense do you tend to receive reliable intuitive impressions?** I receive most of my intuitive flashes through my vision. I literally see in my mind's eye that a client will be wearing a gray jacket, or I see the initial "K" and know that someone whose name begins with that letter will be important to me that day.

- **In what ways do you tend to misinterpret your intuitive impressions?** Are you completely off or does it tend to be a matter of degree?

- **How accurate are your intuitive impressions?** Do you edit them out as "distractions" or do you mistake emotions like hope or fear for detached intuitive impressions?

- **Does your intuition tend to be more accurate with certain subjects than with others?** Perhaps your readings are extremely accurate about the stock market but not about real estate. Perhaps you have a great sense of the general public but a less reliable one of individuals.

- **Does your intuition tend to be more accurate in certain situations than others?** When I'm under the most pressure I'm also my most accurate, but not when I'm panicked. For example, I know that when I'm in a time of financial difficulty, it isn't a time for me to do speculative things. That isn't true of my brother. When he's under financial duress, he does his best investing.

- **Does your intuition tend to be more accurate in certain time frames than others?** Are you most accurate about the past, the present, or the future? Regarding the future, do you tend to be more accurate in the short term or in the long term?

The more you get to know your own intuitive sense, the more you'll know how and when you can rely on it.

ONE PERSON'S RESPONSE

I'm fairly in touch with a number of situations in which my intuitive voice is quite clear. The first is in the early morning, just as I'm waking up. I try to maintain this semidreamlike, semiconscious awareness as long as I can without fully waking up, because my conscious mind hasn't quite kicked in yet and the quality of these intuitive impressions is first-rate. I always "check them out" later, and invariably my hunches are unerring.

Another time my reasoning mind is unable to interfere with my intuitive impressions is, oddly enough, when I'm speaking in front of a group. I am frequently called upon to make public speeches to large audiences. Most people hate speaking in public, but I love to because that's when I get my best ideas. And if I want to focus on my reasoning and turn down my intuitive "receiver," I'll begin typing on my computer. I don't know why, perhaps it's because I type so slowly.

Anyway, I sometimes prepare for these talks, yet I'm always surprised by the often profound insights I blurt out seemingly from nowhere. It's gotten to the point where if I want to use my intuition to solve a problem or to be creative, I'll organize a public talk on the topic. For some reason, speaking to just one or two people doesn't allow me to gain access to the same part of my unconscious.

The quality of my intuitive process is actually markedly different in these situations than it is normally. My "waking up" hunches tend to be fully formed, perhaps because my unconscious has been "cooking" these ideas all night. There's also a kind of fluid calm about them.

My "speaking" hunches, on the other hand, are more fragmentary. They also have a quality I call "speedy thought." One impression instantly leads to another, which instantly leads to another, and so on. Ideas come almost fully hatched.

Despite these differences, my hunches are invariably auditory, rather than visual or physical, and they always seem to come from "someplace else." My hunches at these times—when waking up and in public speaking—are so wonderful that I might even be accused of bragging if I didn't also admit that I don't seem to have anything to do with them. My hunches always seem like gifts I've done nothing to deserve.

DISCUSSION

This student is quite "tuned in" to her intuitive process. You may have experienced something similar to her experience with public speeches if you've ever been troubled by a problem, explained it to someone else, and then right in the middle of speaking, the solution suddenly dawned on you. Notice also that she is aware that both of the situations in which she is conscious of her intuitive impressions are ones in which it's difficult for her conscious mind to interfere—that is, to reason.

BE ESPECIALLY CAREFUL IN TWO SITUATIONS

In addition to the more general ways we can go astray in the intuitive process, there are two times when this is especially likely.

The first is when your emotions are heavily engaged. We spoke earlier about the importance of remaining detached during the intuitive process. Accurate intuitive impressions are usually objective. This is hard to achieve when you're trying to get an intuitive hit on something you feel strongly about, or about which you have strong hopes or fears.

Even if you have no strong emotions one way or the other about something you're doing a reading of, you must be on guard against allowing outside emotional issues to color your interpretations. If your dog just ran away or you had an argument earlier that morning with your best friend, your intuitive reading is likely to be less reliable than usual. This is the purpose of doing body checks before every reading.

The other time you must be suspicious of your intuition is, surprisingly, when your impressions say exactly what your logic or your emotions are telling you! We discussed this earlier under the topic of checks and balances. If what you're intuiting is the same as what you're feeling, or what logic tells you, you can assume you're not using your intuition.

The point is that there should be some agreement between your intuition and your logic or your emotions, but not complete agreement. Remember that these are very different modes of experiencing the world around you.

WHAT DO YOU DO WHEN YOUR INSTINCTS TELL YOU ONE THING AND LOGIC AND "THE FACTS" TELL YOU ANOTHER?

That's the million-dollar question. Consider Alan Greenspan, chairman of the Federal Reserve Board. Few persons in the business world have better access to or a firmer grasp on financial data (or a wetter one—he reads Federal Reserve staff reports in the bathtub before going to work) than he does. According to the *Wall Street Journal*, however, he "ignores staff advice whenever he thinks his personal forecast is better."

Albert Einstein "knew" his theory of relativity was right long before it was proven. When asked by a reporter for his response should an upcoming major experiment fail to confirm his theory, Einstein replied, "Then the facts would be wrong."

〰〰〰

INTUITION IN ACTION

During many years in business, I have learned to rely on my intuitive sense to guide me in selecting whom I should work with and whom I should avoid. One example of this occurred when a high-profile businessman asked me to interview with him regarding strategies to help his company expand its market share.

Upon entering his office for the first time, I felt a vague sensation of discomfort. Our meeting was dynamic and the project was perfect for me, yet when I left his office I had a pounding headache. At first I did not connect the physical symptoms with the fact that this person was highly duplicitous, nor did I consciously realize that I shouldn't be doing business with this individual.

After two more meetings wherein the same physical manifestations occurred (I even became optically dizzy while seated in the conference room of this man's office), I discussed the matter with my husband, who is a highly respected physician. He encouraged me to "listen to my body" and interpret what these sensations were trying to communicate to me.

I realized that my discomfort was signaling that I did not belong in an association with this man, in spite of his outwardly impressive stature. I had read press coverage lauding his accomplishments, and I had heard rave reviews from several people who had known him in the world of commerce. However, my inner voice clearly said that the man's methods of conducting business were questionable, even though I had no tangible evidence of this at the time. Therefore, when he offered me a lucrative position with his company, I declined, saying that I preferred to continue working independently in my own company.

Many months passed, and I often wondered if I had made the right decision after all. I had passed up what seemed to be an incredible opportunity because of my intuition. Over a year later, I learned that this man had been totally unscrupulous and highly destructive in dealing with another company that was revered in its industry. In the process, a side of this man's nature was revealed that had not been known by many before, and it was received with great shock. Because I listened to my gut, I was spared an association with someone who eventually proved to be disingenuous.

~~21~~

How Can I Anticipate
and Overcome Obstacles?
(IT'S POSSIBLE TO SOLVE PROBLEMS
BEFORE THEY ARISE)

An Ounce of Prevention

As the old saying goes, it's worth a pound of cure. Obviously, the best way to "solve" a problem is to prevent it in the first place.

By continually monitoring your business world, and by revisiting the defining questions of your business world (pages 29 and 42–4) regularly, you will be alert to potential warning signs almost before they occur. Once intuition is part of your reasoning and living process, you'll know when something is "off" simply because your intuitive pulse changes. When your pulse alerts you to a change, you can then combine your intuition with your logical and empirical techniques to evaluate the change and take action.

The great thing about intuition is that you troubleshoot for the future today, giving you plenty of time in which to respond.

EXERCISE 25
STRAIGHT TALK

The question to this exercise appears on page 187. You are asked to make a yes or no prediction about a particular event and to create a time line surrounding it. Allow yourself to use your senses to help you answer this question intuitively in a conversational tone while at the

---

same time establishing a time line. In other words, you will be receiving an intuitive impression and translating it (if it needs translation) immediately into dialogue. Read the examples before you do the exercise.

ONE PERSON'S READING AND INTERPRETATION

This will come close to happening in July. The other party will lose interest. They will try to stall and then they will leave. Everything will be resolved by the end of the summer. It will be harder and harder to get in contact with this person. This should be starting now. This will not happen.

I see a possibility of this in May and a definite yes by December. It will be preceded by a boost in sales caused by a sudden interest in a stagnant product. I feel that the items have to do with women. It feels big.

Oh, boy, be careful of what you ask for because you may get it. I see a yes much sooner than expected. It will be preceded by a short trip to a warm place. I see June. You'll laugh at how easy this is and how much energy you have expended in an obvious and wonderful outcome that needed so much less of your time to make it happen.

DISCUSSION

If you get a "no" when you do this exercise yourself, do some troubleshooting now so you can take corrective steps to ensure success.

THE ROOT CAUSE OF MOST BUSINESS DIFFICULTIES

Not frequently scanning your ever-changing situation will certainly allow problems to develop. But problems may develop even if you are continually troubleshooting. After all, you're not going to notice everything affecting your business.

So when a problem does arise, it is almost always caused by a lack of integrity between one or more spheres in your business world. Perhaps

Exercise 25. Will I be able to reach my current goal? If so, when, and what events will precede it?

you are no longer responding to the changing needs of your team. Or the team is not responding well to changes in the business environment.

The erosion of integrity, in turn, is often caused by a breakdown in communication during times of change. One sphere is expressing needs that another is either not meeting or isn't perceived as meeting.

If your company isn't vital, there's a lapse in its integrity. It's as simple as that. You can sell ice to Inuit Eskimos if your integrity is intact. You make the market, and your market—your company—is a reflection of what you are. It's a mirror.

And sometimes you've changed—and your job or your company is no longer responding to your needs and values. As we discussed earlier, your unconscious will make it difficult for you to succeed in a job or company that isn't important to you in a profound way.

How do you revitalize yourself or your company? First you must diagnose the precise nature of the integrity breakdown. You do that by asking questions.

YOU CAN ASK PEOPLE ON YOUR TEAM OR IN YOUR BUSINESS ENVIRONMENT

If you expect people who know you to be honest—especially during times of trouble—you're dreaming.

So let everyone talk anonymously. Don't just request contributions to the company suggestion box or distribute "yet another survey" filled with trite—and dishonest—questions like "Who's doing a good job and who isn't?" or "How can we improve our products and services in a total quality way?"

Give your people a chance to vent. Really encourage frankness by calling them "bitch sheets." Tell them to pick on your coworkers! Don't ask too many questions, and make sure they're funny.

Leave lots of space for your respondents. Then present the results creatively, in a skit, for example, so people can begin to work on solutions to the problems they've aired.

YOU CAN EVEN ASK STRANGERS OR OTHER PEOPLE WHO "KNOW NOTHING ABOUT YOUR BUSINESS"

It's sometimes difficult for people you deal with to feel free to give honest feedback, but strangers are not as inhibited. What's more, because they have no logical or factual background on your situation, they're more likely to give their intuitive responses.

They may be puzzled and ask you to describe the details of your situation. Give them a few insignificant ones and then apologize—"That's all I know"—so they aren't tempted to "figure out" what the problem is. Then gently press them for answers. If they balk at your request—"How do you expect me to solve your problem if I don't know anything about it?"—invite them to make something up.

You Can Use I-Mode to Become the Business and Ask Yourself Questions

Intuitive doctors and healers often diagnose the cause of an illness with "symptom dialogue," where your tumor talks to you and you talk to your tumor. "It's all that fat you're eating," your tumor tells you.

If your company's health is in question, you can have a similar dialogue with it or any aspect of it (the marketing department, or finance, for instance). Simply become your business, using our techniques, and ask yourself what's wrong.

This is an excellent group exercise for your team members in a meeting. Individuals can take turns becoming the business (or the supplier, or the market, or whatever sphere you choose) and responding to questions from the group. It's important for the person becoming the business to speak intuitively rather than telling you what he or she thinks logically. Everyone should be encouraged to "make something up" if they don't know the answer. As always, such off-the-cuff remarks are amazingly accurate.

EXERCISE 26
TALK TO ME

Imagine that your business is actually a person sitting across a table from you. Allow yourself to see, feel, smell, and hear your business. First, describe your business. What does it look like? How could it look better?

Next, ask it the following questions: What's wrong with you? What do you want? How can I help?

Last, let your business ask *you* questions. Respond to them.

You can also role-play this with people in your company (or with friends). Allow one person to be the business and describe himself and then question him.

Keep in mind that you can do this exercise from other points of view. You can use I-mode to become a business and then question the market, for example.

This exercise seems silly until you've done it once, after which you'll realize that it is incredibly effective.

ASK OTHERS—BUT THINK FOR YOURSELF!

Sources you rely upon can often be your Achilles' heel because you are patterned to trust them whether or not they are trustworthy. The worst mistakes I have made in business I have made through relying on the perceptions of people I trusted even when my gut told me they were wrong.

I recently made one such "disastrous move" on the advice of a friend. I didn't do the logical thing, which was to research her advice. And I didn't do the intuitive thing, which was to follow my gut (which told me to mistrust this recommendation).

Because I wanted to trust my friend's judgment, and because I wanted a quick solution to a difficult problem, her suggestion seemed to be "just what I was looking for." I received many more intuitive clues that I should listen to my own good judgment, and I ignored them, which, ultimately, in the eleventh hour got me into a mess.

With perfect hindsight I realized that I had been working against my own perceptions the whole time. I had so badly wanted to believe that she was right that my emotions interfered both with my perceptions and my judgment of those perceptions. Thank heavens that I had also been preparing for the mess the whole time (without being totally aware I was doing so) or I would have been in a real pickle! You will find that the more you use your intuition, the more your intuitive information will prepare you for the messes you don't want to see even when you are not consciously paying attention to the information!

For me, this situation highlighted the importance in this book of emphasizing that you need to know what your agenda is and the sources of your information so that they can be viewed dispassionately in order to make sound decisions.

Intuition helps us do this, if we listen to it. We often know that we are not listening to it when we hear only what we want to hear!

You Cannot "Become" the Problem If You View It as a Threat

You'll remember from our discussion of enemies that viewing something as a threat limits your ability to "become" it. This, in turn, limits your ability to gain useful knowledge or insights about its needs and how you can respond to them effectively. Indeed, an effective response often not only eliminates the enemy but turns the enemy into an ally.

Similarly, a "problem" is often a matter of perception. If you are able to open yourself up to it, you may discover useful possibilities.

Let's say you're the president of a clothing company and you've just been informed by certified mail that your company is a takeover target. This is a hostile takeover, so it would almost certainly mean your ouster.

Now, your first impulse, of course, might be to ask, "How can I neutralize this threat?" This isn't a bad starting point. I say starting point because if you can stop viewing the situation as a threat, you free yourself to ask other questions, like, "Could this be a good thing?"

Let's see how this questioning process might proceed. You might neutralize the threat by pointing out to the other company that all your manufacturing equipment is fifty years old, and that some of your employee contracts in Europe can't be broken and are bleeding the profits.

And in pursuing this line you see that the other party also has European plants with similar labor contract problems. And maybe you notice that their product could be manufactured in their own plant at a lower cost if they were willing to switch seasons with yours. Maybe you could create a working relationship with them, and give them a certain amount of stock in your company without giving up a controlling interest.

This also suggests other ideas. Perhaps with your help the other party could enter markets that were previously closed to it. You get the idea. The point of this example is to demonstrate that by neutralizing a threat, you've actually created an opportunity.

One of the great things about the intuitive process is that it allows you to shift your point of view in real ways. And the more easily you can change your point of view, the more easily you can respond in flexible ways to changing situations.

By now you have a solid sense of where your integrity meets that of your company and your market. The next exercise will refine that sense even further.

EXERCISE 27
TOWER OF BABEL

This is a blind exercise. Your responses to the situations below will actually answer questions on page 193, so record your impressions even if they don't seem relevant—they probably won't make sense until you interpret them later.

Situation 1: Imagine that you are standing in the middle of the Tower of Babel, voices bouncing all around you. You are the only person there who knows that a major earthquake is about to hit in five minutes, leveling the structure. There is no way for you to get through the crowd to safety if you don't organize and direct them in some way.

What do you do?

Situation 2: Imagine that you have a bad sunburn.

What do you use to relieve the pain, and in the meantime, what must you avoid?

Situation 3: Imagine that you are in a strange kitchen and you'd like to make some soup.

What, if anything, is missing, and where will you find it?

Situation 4: Finally, imagine that you have safely ushered the people from the Tower of Babel to a long table and are to serve them the soup you wanted to prepare. Were you able to make the soup? How do you get them to sit down at the table? How do they respond to you in your sunburned state? Do they like it? What now is missing?

ONE PERSON'S RESPONSE

I touch the person next to me and hold my finger to my lips in a gesture of quiet. Point in a direction and then touch another person and another until they are all touching each other and going in the same direction, calmly, through touch.

Wind, people grabbing me, having to move too quickly, not having access to salves and soft materials.

I have a good sense of how people's kitchens are set up. I think that containers would be the hardest thing for me to find.

I have served them the soup, but I've forgotten the spoons. Wait. They can pick the bowls up and drink, back-to-nature style. They like the soup, but they want some bread. They look to me and I find some in the storeroom. They like me and want to embrace me, but I need to find a nice way to keep my distance so that they don't irritate my sunburn. I do this by singing to them from a distance.

To interpret your impressions, see the questions at the bottom of this page.

THE EVALUATION

I need to find a way in which our "ideas" touch the hearts of the market. I might do this by toning down the presentation a bit and focusing on instructions and values.

I can't be buffeted by other products and opinions. I need to move slowly on the upcoming projects and make sure that I have the resources structured before I begin.

I need to concentrate on how I get the product to the market. I might want to stay low tech in this area. I might concentrate on creating something useful and traditional to accompany my product. Oh, I already have it in the "storeroom." I'll have to think about what that might be. Radio might be a good way to promote it.

Exercise 27:
What are the solutions to the difficulties with your market?
What are the solutions to the difficulties with yourself?
What are the solutions to the difficulties with your company?
How can the problems of integrity be resolved?

DISCUSSION

You can change the scenarios in this exercise to suit any situation. This is a good exercise to do with a group. Comparing the information generated often creates new perspectives on the same issue. You will be surprised by how many different ways the same answer can be expressed.

━━━━

INTUITION IN ACTION
TAKING ACTION BEFORE THE AX FALLS

I consulted once with someone in a top-level position at a major chain of department stores. All the top executives knew the chain was going to be acquired, they just didn't know by whom. As a result, they were extremely nervous and bailing out in droves because they all thought they were going to be fired.

I told my client what company would buy the chain. I also told her that she knew the person who would become the CEO of her division. I gave her an initial of that person.

She knew immediately who I was talking about, so she began to network with her contacts at that company. Eventually, she sent that person to me as a client. You can imagine how surprised he was, since no one even knew there was an offer on the table to buy out the company.

━━━━

DISCUSSION

The point of this story is that by using intuition, my client was able to approach her situation proactively. She could develop better relationships with her contacts at the acquiring company and get a sense of how this situation would figure into her long-term plans. She didn't have to feel that panicky "How am I going to save my job?" feeling. Instead, she could calmly ask herself, "Do I want to save my job? Where do I see myself a few years from now? How could this acquisition help further my plans?" She is on her own now and extremely successful in both her career and her life.

It is rare that life follows a straight line. There are always detours. Yet these detours can improve your marketing power by adding to your perspective. With intuition you can anticipate when those times will be, prepare for them creatively, and use them to create greater strength.

If you see a barrier, there is always a way around it, through it, over it, or, as a last resort, a way to reframe it positively.

~~~~~~

INTUITION IN ACTION
MAKE IT HAPPEN

The problem of using intuition has several prongs. First, as I'm often painfully aware, is separating out the background noise from what may be intuitive perception. We often have all kinds of thoughts buzzing through our heads, and it takes a bit of work and self-control to get to the right frequency.

You can't make intuition happen by trying harder. As Buckminster Fuller once said, you need to "go in to go out." Or do the opposite of trying, whatever that might be.

In my experience, it seems to work more like E-mail: You send off the question, and when the intuition gets around to it, it answers. Which is why in my case, I'm more likely to get certain types of intuitive reactions when I wake up, or when I take a shower.

Which raises another question: What can be known by using the intuitive faculty? Maybe it's just about everything. Or maybe not. Even if it's only partly everything, it's still pretty exciting. And accessible. Learning to be intuitive is probably not so different from learning to play golf, or ride a bicycle, or read. It's just a set of skills that many of us haven't been using habitually.

There's a saying in Zen Buddhism that to point to the moon, you need a finger, but that you should never mistake the pointing finger for the moon. Intuition is not the moon, but it does make a pretty good finger.

~~~~~~

~22~

USING INTUITION TO PREDICT THE STOCK MARKET: A CASE STUDY

PUTTING IT ALL TOGETHER

Now we're going to see how we can apply all the steps we've learned, together with our work on I-mode, to predict the stock market.

The stock market provides an excellent arena for intuitive practice. A company can report record sales and the price is just as likely to plummet as it is to soar. The explanation for this is that the information you are relying on may already have been "discounted by the market"; by the time something becomes news, all the "movers and shakers" have already acted on it, making it too late for everyone else.

The stock market is also a place where information is not always reliable, and where it isn't clear who knows more about a stock, the buyer or the seller.

The major problem with investing, of course, is the enormous difficulty of maintaining intuitive detachment when you have money riding on the line.

YOU CAN USE ALL OUR TECHNIQUES

Of course, a time line really helps here, as do blind readings and creating metaphors to ensure detached readings. You'll recall the apple exercise we did way at the beginning.

The Importance of Precise Targeting

Whichever technique or combination of techniques you use, know precisely what your intuition is targeting.

First, remember that you predict the price of the stock, not what happens to the company. The company can be doing very well but its stock price can still go down. That used to baffle me when I was first doing this. I'd feel a surge and a strengthening in the company, then the stock price would go down 10 percent—whoops!

Second, know your time frame. Are you targeting tomorrow's price or next month's?

Third, know the basis of measurement. The change in stock price can be measured from today's closing price to tomorrow's opening price, or from tomorrow's opening price to tomorrow's closing price. It doesn't matter which one you choose so long as you consciously make a choice.

Fourth, decide what you mean by up, down, or unchanged. If you think the Dow Jones average will close down slightly tomorrow and it closes up by .01 percentage points, you're not too far off the mark.

Finally, if you are following other economic indicators, make sure you frame your target precisely. If you're following government employment statistics, for example (an important indicator in the stock and bond markets), you should be asking your intuition not whether employment will increase or decrease, but whether the government's *report* will indicate an increase or a decrease.

So remember to keep your focus on the target.

EXERCISE 28
I-MODE AND THE STOCK MARKET

To keep things manageable, select three stocks you want to follow. Pick three stocks, or three of any commodity, like sugar or mutual funds, which have prices posted daily.

First, use all your senses to look at each stock. Allow yourself to become this stock. Make it your "I." Not just your mind and your thoughts, but your breath, your body, and all of your senses.

Then make a formal decision to make yourself "I the price," not "I the company." Remember, it's always important to know your target.

Use your intuition now to describe the company. If you can describe the company, you won't confuse it with its price. You may get some information on the future of this company that will help you determine its price.

As you do so, consider the following questions from the point of view of today:

- How are you feeling?
- What are you looking for?
- When will you find it?
- How do you need it presented to you to make you want it?
- What is your favorite thing about it?
- What do you like the least?

Then look ahead a day (or a week, or whatever time frame you're choosing):

- In what ways have you changed?
- What have you been doing?
- What else has gone on in the world?
- How did you do last year?

Then, based on this information, ask yourself, "Will the stock price in this company go up or down tomorrow?"

Based on your impressions, how and by how much will the stock price change?

ONE PERSON'S READING

I am this company. I feel strong, but I also feel that a part of me, my left side, is falling off. I don't know what to do to it anymore, but I feel as if my right side is getting stronger and stronger and will be really strong in about three or four months. I feel something new coming out.

I'm excited about it. It won't initially have the effect I had hoped for, but then it will become a really big hit. As it is a big hit, another company becomes a part of me. I can feel an element added; I think it's another company.

Based on these impressions, I expect the stock price to increase.

Discussion

It's important to get feedback after you do your reading. If the stock price went down when you believed it would rise, go back and look at your notes and see why.

Look also at the magnitude of the change and the timing. Maybe you should take another look at how you're interpreting your symbolism. In our previous example, the investor focused on the strengthening of one "side" of the company despite a weakening of the other, and interpreted that in a positive way. Perhaps the symbolism was instead pointing to the imbalance between the "left" and "right," which would suggest a negative outcome. Now that the investor has this feedback, he won't make the same mistake.

Again: Know Your Strengths and Limitations

When you use intuition in the stock market, as elsewhere, you must learn your specific strengths and limitations as they refer to this particular area. Consider the following questions:

- In which time frames are you most accurate? In which time frame are you least accurate? I'm more accurate day to day than over longer time periods.
- Which markets do you intuit most accurately? I have an easier time with commodities than stocks because their price movements seem more immediate to me.
- In which situations are you most accurate? Evaluating companies themselves (their earnings prospects, for example) is somewhat easier than stock prices. I tend to do well with initial public offerings.
- In what situations are you least accurate? I can never do financial readings when I'm suffering angst. The message that keeps coming through to me is, "You're going to be annihilated, you're going to starve." That's not a place where you can look for a gain. However, it is a place where you can get someone else to do a reading for you.
- What biases do you notice? I'm really bad once I know a stock's name because I fall in love with words. I'm a writer. I know I fall in love with words. I know I prefer "S's" and "R's."

- Which techniques work best for you to gain access to the financial markets? For me, if my finger goes up, the price is going up. I know this sounds stupid, but it works for me. It's amazing how much you can rely on what your body senses. Does your eyebrow twitch? If so, does it twitch up or down? Check your body's reaction against actual results for a week, and you'll be surprised at how accurate you are. You just have to get in closer touch with what your body is saying.

MY INTUITIVE LESSON

I recently taught a class of some sixty students in Toronto. As practice, at one point everyone paired off to give and receive blind readings by using the envelope technique (actually just with papers folded over several times). One of the students, an investor, had given his partner a piece of paper with the following question: "What will happen to Bre-X?" His partner had trouble getting a fix on this question so they called me over for help.

Bre-X, I should mention, was being followed by every other Canadian at the time. It was a gold stock that had plummeted a few days earlier when the company announced that their previously announced "major gold discovery" might be "smaller than expected." It wasn't clear whether the mining company would recover, continue to decline, or even declare bankruptcy.

I went to their table and opened the sheet of paper (so his partner wouldn't see the question). I whispered that the question was worded too vaguely and suggested the following revision: "Will the price of Bre-X be higher on this May sixth than it is today, April twelfth?" I picked May sixth "out of a hat"—or so I thought—to give the question a precise time horizon.

I gave the new question, again hidden, to the investor's partner. This time she had the clear sense of a downward spiraling motion, which she interpreted as a "no."

On the spur of the moment, I decided to turn the question into a group exercise. I asked all the participants to close their eyes so that they would not see each other's responses (a useful technique, incidentally, to use in meetings) when responding to the question I held in my hand. I then asked all those who would answer "yes" to the question to raise their right arms.

Every student in the class—the investor and his partner abstaining—raised his or her hand to indicate yes! That was odd, since the investor's partner had gotten such a clear impression of the opposite.

Who was correct? Well, I was curious, too, so on May sixth I immediately opened my morning paper to the business section. I was surprised to see the headline. May sixth, the date I had selected "just at random," was the very day the company would announce that there was little or no gold in its "huge mine." In the ensuing investor panic, the stock instantly became almost worthless.

This is an illustration not just of how effective blind readings can be, but of how important it is to target your time frame for your intuition as precisely as possible.

Why was the class wrong and the investor's partner so accurate? I learned two important lessons from the experience.

First, people will "bend" their perceptions according to the expectations of the "leader," even when they are not conscious of what those expectations are. Remember that as the group's leader I asked them to indicate a positive response by raising their hands.

Second, we all think like a herd even when that thinking is wrong. I am now even more conscious of the way I phrase questions, and of the way I conduct meetings.

〜〜〜〜〜

DAILY PRACTICE
PAPER TRADING

The stock market or any financial market is an excellent target for daily quick-hit exercises because you get immediate feedback in terms of direction and magnitude as well as timing.

You don't need to invest in the market to do this exercise. I'm not encouraging you to buy stocks, and I'm certainly not encouraging beginners to speculate.

"Paper trading" is the term brokers and other professionals use in the industry to "pretend" that they've actually invested money so they can practice their trading. It's enormously more difficult, of course, when you have hard cash on the line and your emotions can swing up and down as wildly as the Dow Jones average.

You can pick a stock, or an industry, or a commodity, or one of each. It doesn't matter. Practice different time frames. You may not be so accurate on a daily basis, but you may be extremely accurate on a weekly or monthly basis.

〰〰〰

～23～

How Can I Stay Ahead of My Market to Respond to Changing Needs and Opportunities?
(Success in the Marketplace is Not a Static Thing)

It is never too late to be what you might have been.
—George Eliot

Maintaining the Balance Point of Your Integrity in a Changing World

As your business world changes, you must be ever sensitive to maintaining the balance point of the many needs to which you must respond. Yet it is not always easy to change, especially if you have had a great deal of success with what you are currently doing. We tend to have a set way of dealing with events. We fall into habits, into comfortable patterns that—for the moment, at least—work. Changing ourselves isn't easy; it's also a little scary.

All the elements need to be able to be called into action harmoniously. We're not just talking about values; we're talking about the business machine and how it functions. If you think of the human body as a machine, when your respiration is high, your digestion is low. But if you eat something, your digestive tract needs to spring into action. So integrity is the ability of each part of the whole to respond to the needs of the organism in the environment. We're talking about corporate health.

Here's an example. You have too large a product development team, and you sense that you need to better market what you have. But you can't downsize because if you successfully market what you have in the next few months, you'll need that development team to be able to respond. So you frame it for the development team: "We need to work on creating the market for what you've developed. In the interim, we are going to need to redeploy some of you to other areas." At the same time, focus on a totally different part of your business that has the support of your development staff. In this way you are effectively responding to the needs of your team as well as your needs so that you are both better able to respond to those of the market.

This example illustrates two important concepts. First, there must be a consensus of integrity within a company. You cannot impose integrity on your team or your market. And second, even if a proposal initially appears to upset the balance point, if wrong it can be reframed and sometimes improved so that it is in keeping with the identity of the company.

BE WILLING TO ADAPT

Sometimes, successful individuals or businesses stumble or fall because they fail to monitor their changing business world. When I was a child growing up in New York City, every neighborhood had numerous small food shops: the local butcher, the local baker, the local fish market, the local greengrocer. These mom-and-pop specialty food shops have now, by and large, disappeared.

Why? Because their owners did not respond to the changing needs of their market. Those businesses were replaced by businesses that were responsive to those changing needs: either large supermarkets, or small delicatessens that are like mini-supermarkets and offer convenience and accessibility.

How did their market change? Consumers, either because of shifting demographics, or changing neighborhoods, or the changing nature of work and family, had less time for everything, including shopping. Their market wanted fast, convenient, one-stop shopping. People no longer had time to go to lots of different shops. They no longer had time for the personal relationships they had once had with shop owners.

Enter the large supermarket—which offered the convenience of one-stop shopping with an even greater selection of foods—and the mini-markets—which were able to charge a premium to the market by offering greater convenience even with less selection.

Had the baker not been so invested in being a "baker," or the butcher "a butcher," these businesses might have perceived a need for a small specialty store, one that enticed the consumer with the best bakery or meat section in the neighborhood.

SCANNING YOUR BUSINESS WORLD FOR OPPORTUNITIES

In the same way that monitoring your business world by continually asking the defining questions allows you to troubleshoot potential problems, it also allows you to catch opportunities the moment they arise. Too often individuals and businesses get stuck in problem-solving mode, but it's just as important to exploit opportunities. And because your business environment and your market's needs are continually changing, there are always new opportunities arising.

Even in a bad stock market, there's a way to make a living. Structure people's debt, for one thing! There is no such thing as a bad market for the good salesperson. If you know that all the oranges in Florida will die, then maybe you should sell imported oranges. If people lose their taste for oranges, go into apples.

CONTINUALLY TROUBLESHOOT YOUR ENVIRONMENT— EVEN IF EVERYTHING'S GREAT

Sometimes everything in your career or in your company is on a roll. Things seem to be just falling into your lap. So you take your integrity with your business environment for granted. You relax your vigilance in watching for warning signs. Perhaps a hidden agenda pops up and you begin to sabotage your success.

And, of course, before you know it, you've hit the wall.

But integrity is something you must maintain consciously, because it's so easy for individuals and businesses to mistake accidental integrity for actually being in touch with their business environment.

Here's an example. Someone who loves children decides that what the world needs is environmentally correct day-care centers. He hasn't gone through the process of becoming his environment and asking himself what it wants. So he invests his life savings in an environmentally correct day-care center—and it's a smashing success.

Unfortunately, this success just cuts him off from his market and business environment even further. "Boy, I'm good," he says, congratulating himself.

So instead of continually monitoring his environment to ask it what it wants, he decides to plunge ahead and open a chain of such centers. His bank loan is approved and he opens ten centers in the next few years.

At first he doesn't notice the drop-off in attendance because total revenues have been increasing. But before long, his accountant tells him that although total revenues have doubled, the average revenue of each center has fallen through the floor.

And a year later he declares bankruptcy.

DON'T FORGET THAT YOUR NEEDS AND VALUES CHANGE, TOO

Remember that things in your business world continually change. So do you. That means you need to continually reevaluate your situation, not every day, but frequently. I reevaluate my business plan just about every week. "What do I want?" is always the first question I ask. What interferes with my ability to organize my assets and resources the most is that I change, but I don't reevaluate my goal.

Once I wanted economic security. Now I have that. If I kept striving for that, it would be an empty goal. Ultimately, my unconscious would sabotage me. So I reevaluate. Now I want greater economic security, but I also want a platform on which to make a difference in the world. I haven't yet specified how I plan to do that, nor do I feel it is critical that I do so now (purpose being more important than outcome). It's important to learn which parts of your goal are fixed and which parts are replaceable. Keep track of those changes so you can move faster, with less baggage.

~~~~~~

DAILY PRACTICE
MAINTAINING YOUR FINGER ON THE
PULSE OF YOUR CHANGING MARKET

Don't forget to do your body check. Write down on a piece of paper "how my market is changing."

Allow your focus to move away from the question and take a moment to allow yourself to notice all of your thoughts and sensations (about anything at all) and record them. Speak or write continuously for a few minutes; don't stop for a second.

When you have finished recording your impressions, put this exercise aside. At some point during the day, return to what you have recorded. Notice the tone, the details, where your attention went, what you needed to express to "get going."

You will find bits of information to help you anticipate the needs of all your business dimensions. Often, when you have put down your pen or turned off your tape recorder, your thoughts will come together for you in a phrase or a sentence.

It is especially helpful to view these collectively at the end of the week, both for their intuitive content and their empirical and emotive content. They will give you a pretty good sense of where things are headed.

~~~~~~

CONTINUALLY STRIVE TO IMPROVE YOUR RESPONSIVENESS

Your success in business depends on how well you find a fit between what you have and want to offer and what someone else wants or needs. Remember that your market's needs are always changing, often without its awareness. So if you truly want to succeed in business, you must not only meet your market's expectations, you must anticipate and exceed them!

Lay out all your journal notes and transcripts in front of you. Divide them into two piles—one for the personal, one for the career. Read every word of both, jotting down any instinctive reactions in the margins. Then lay them aside for a moment and take a five-minute break to clear your head.

Blend this information with your own perceptions, which you uncovered in the "I" exercise. Who is this person who is you? Record a brief description of yourself based on all of this information.

Armed with this new information, though, who could you be and what could you do? Go ahead, ask! "Who could I be and what could I do to be even more successful than I am today?" Enhancing your personal power means that you consciously fine-tune and take advantage of all your assets.

When I did this exercise, many years ago, I was surprised at how generously people interpreted what I thought of as my defects. "Shyness," "blunt to a fault," and "sometimes overbearing" were interpreted as "modest," "willing to give feedback," "generous," and "a natural leader." Some of the things I thought of as a given about myself I had some shocking feedback on. I took all of the information and looked at my traits from a different perspective and got both a better grasp of who I was and a clearer picture of how I was perceived, as well as the possibilities for embodying some different and useful "I's." The following exercise gives all of the parts that "you" comprise information and permission to be more creative and intuitive about how you see yourself, others, and your market.

EXERCISE 29
EVERY DAY IN EVERY WAY, I GET BETTER AND BETTER

What is the first thing you see right now? Describe it in detail. As you do so, consider the following questions:

- What or who does it remind you of?
- How would you like to change it?
- Where would it look best?
- What would you like to do with it?

ONE PERSON'S READING

I see a shelf full of books, half of which is hidden by a Chinese screen. It reminds me of a Native American. A warrior, a hunter, a gatherer, a husband, a wise man, a leader, a supporter. The self-sufficiency of being. I would like to remove the screen so that there could be a more open feeling. The screen looks best exactly where it is.

THE INTERPRETATION

My ability to integrate knowledge is my strength and I need to use it more. I tend to be withdrawn and I need to uncover more of myself to make the strides I want to in my career. Only my closest friends know how funny I am. I could use this more on the job.

My company is also understated and needs to be more out there. We have had plenty of opportunity, but our emphasis has been on product development, which may be unwise since many of our opportunities fall under marketing. I appear self-sufficient and able to protect and sustain things: projects, ideas, staff, and so on. I think this makes me a good manager. This wasn't part of the question my company was focusing its energies on, which was whether to develop new markets in Southeast Asia.

CONTINUALLY STRIVE TO IMPROVE YOUR COMPANY'S RESPONSIVENESS

Let's look at the assets for your corporate "I." Let's pretend your corporation is a discount department store. "Excellent prices" is one comment. "Really friendly people" is another. "Dedicated customer service." What could you do or be to be even more successful than you are today?

If you were Sam Walton, you would make the one decision that would guarantee your success: You would build warehouses around the country so that every one of your Wal-Mart stores would be no more than half a day away from a reliable source of supply. As a result, your customers would always have up-to-date merchandise.

If you were Michael Dell, you would turn the computer industry on its ear by selling computers through the mail. How would you do it? By making one critical decision: not to make any of the parts yourself. Instead, you'd buy parts from computer manufacturers and assemble the units only when the orders came in. Then you'd rigorously test for reliability so that the computers mailed out were never returned. Today, Dell Computer is a model for the industry, and Michael Dell is a billionaire.

What is the one action you could intuit today that would create a breakthrough for your business?

MY EXPERIMENT READING APPLE COMPUTER CORPORATION

As an example of how to use intuition to revitalize a company, I had planned to discuss Apple Computer. Mind you, I know next to nothing about computers, but I do like my Mac. I like it precisely because I don't have to know anything about computers to use it, which I do almost exclusively for word processing. I'm not like a lot of people I know who manage their entire lives by computer. If I did, I would never be able to figure out how to retrieve it!

So, on Sunday, March 9, 1997, I sat down with a friend and a tape recorder to record my intuitive impressions about what Apple Computer should do to improve its business. People had told me the company was having difficulties, and I didn't want it to fail because then I might actually have to learn something about computers! My reading was supposed to be a brief overview that I would later use as the basis for a more in-depth intuitive investigation.

I used I-mode to embody the company and perceive it intuitively with all my senses. What follows is my reading, verbatim, without any editing. Again, I had not intended to publish this reading, so you see it with all its rambling digressions, incomplete sentences, and questionable syntax. Also keep in mind that I am experienced at interpreting my impressions as I report them, a skill you are still developing.

MY READING

I'm Apple. First, I'm going to tell you about myself. I've diversified too much. But I've diversified all under one umbrella. So I'm spilling out with all these confusing products, and it's just falling overboard. I don't really have a goal anymore. I'm dealing with a market that's much more computer literate than the market that started out. And my price points are too high.

I need a really great . . . I need to get kind of the low-end educational part of my company going again. Like an apple with a stem handle that kids can take to school . . . that's also a beeper . . . so parents can get in touch with them. . . . And where . . . that is . . . a computer that can do a couple of things . . . something cheap to produce . . . I don't know . . . $150, $200. . . . Just start. . . . I need my logo to mean something again.

I need to find a way to get rid of my old product. Because my . . . the strongest thing I could do right now, since the problem in the market right now is that people don't buy things because they think next week something better is going to come out . . . is to take an old product and let it be just as good. Let it be versatile. You don't need this. We make computers that last forever, you know?

Go into businesses and find businesses that are using the old Mac system . . . you know, fifteen-year-old Mac systems . . . and it's still working and it's still great. Because we respond to people, and not to things you don't need to know about. I think that's what Apple has right now . . . that their oldest system is still okay.

And I think it needs a character of people. . . . I think that actually Apple should diversify into not so technical things, to capture the young market, who will soon be the computer buyers. So Apple might want to do a push on . . . a young market. Student information education. An approach . . . and books, supplies . . . market some low-end things.

They might want to do a push on office programs so that you can really hire somebody who's not computer literate and they can still use it. So Instant Secretary. How to make anyone into an instant secretary. So people can use their old computers on. . . . And I would still, you know, sell what's been produced. I think they need to get rid of stuff.

And I think they need to, in a sense, agree on a model. Have fewer models, and agree on a model. Create technology that upgrades the model. Like you can take a screen off the keyboard for the home computers . . . why don't they create that kind of compatibility, where you bring in your processor and we'll turn it into a new one, because we don't want you to have to keep buying new computers . . . like those old nasty other companies. . . . We want you to buy a computer and fall in love with it, and that computer will last. But we'll make money off of you every year, because we'll be upgrading it . . . the screen. . . . Do you know what I'm saying?

They can put on a new screen. There are two pieces. They flip up. That's the story. . . . Make it compatible. . . . Someone will steal the idea right away, but Apple would be responsible for it. You know, let's stop screwing the consumer, for God's sake. You know, you need a new computer every year to keep up.

APPLE'S SUBSEQUENT ANNOUNCEMENT

I didn't think anything more about these impressions until I happened to pick up *The New York Times* a month later, on April, 10, 1997. What should I see but an eight-page ad from Apple Computer talking about new products the company was introducing. Here is how the ad read, in part:

> The eMate™ 300 . . . is the first computer that was specifically designed for students. It's small, light, and rugged. Even the shape and colors are just what kids want. It also happens to be affordable, so computers get into the hands of more kids.
>
> Only Apple has built a computer that runs both Mac OS and Windows . . . Introducing the Power Macintosh 7300/180 PC Compatible. Now, with the touch of a button, you can go from using the Mac OS to using Windows 95 or Windows 3.1 or even DOS. . . . Because inside the PowerMac 7300, there's an actual PC. Complete with a 166 MHz Pentium microprocessor. So you can run Windows and Mac applications at the same time . . . it's just like you went out and bought both a PC and a Mac. Because, well, you did.

Oish! I said, they're ruining my chapter! How can I demonstrate the power of intuition to turn a company around if the company adopts half of my plan before my book even gets published?

AN INTERESTING REVIEW

There's more. The April 15, 1997, *New York Times* included a column of Stephen Manes's review of Apple's Newton Messagepad 2000.

> The Messagepad 2000 is a direct descendant of the original Newton, the pen-based hand-held computer widely ridiculed for its perversely

hilarious attempts at turning people's block printing into computerized text.

To solve that problem, Apple had added—what else?—a keyboard. You can still use the "stylus," as the pen is called, if you want to write by hand. But when accuracy is crucial, like for phone numbers and addresses, "the system helpfully pops up an on-screen keyboard on which you can tap in the data."

Compare that with my original reading: *Create technology that upgrades the model. You can take a screen off the keyboard for the home computers.*

Admittedly, they're not exactly "taking a screen off the keyboard." But they did separate it from the keyboard, an idea they could have come to had they had the same intuitive impression.

Manes goes on to report that the Messagepad 2000 points the way toward "a similar machine with a more accessible user interface and a built-in keyboard [that] could begin a very interesting new product category: lightweight but heavy-duty replacements for fat laptops."

Again, compare that with my original reading: *A computer that can do a couple of things.*

ANOTHER ANNOUNCEMENT FROM APPLE

Then, on April 17, 1997, the head of Apple Computer himself weighed in. There, on page B3 of *The Wall Street Journal*, was a full-page letter from the chairman and chief executive officer, Dr. Gil Amelio. Here is what he wrote, in part:

> The excitement will continue with the products we have in the pipeline. Mac OS 8, expected to ship this summer, will further widen the gap between the Mac OS and the rest of the computer industry in terms of ease of use. Its radical new enhancements will make it even easier to navigate the Internet, to work with PCs, to set up a server and to enable average users—without the help of computer experts— to do things they never thought they could with a computer.
>
> We are simplifying, refocusing, getting back to fundamentals. The results show in our products and, with your continued support, should begin to show in our business results soon.

POINTS OF AGREEMENT

Let's review the points of correspondence between my intuitive impressions of what Apple should do and what the company actually did.

First, cost. The price of the eMate 300 is less than $800, according to a news release, which is remarkable considering that most portables are $1,500 and up. My price point of $150 to $200 was considerably lower. This may be a product yet to be created (or put on the market) or I might have used the numbers as my intuition's way of telling me the price would be low and mistaken the symbol for the price.

Let's compare other similarities point by point:

A computer that can do a couple of things.
Sounds like the Power Mac 7300/180 to me.

I need my logo to mean something again.
Dr. Amelio pledges "100% commitment" to that goal.

Take an old product and let it be just as good. Let it be just as versatile.
The Power Mac is now as versatile as any computer on the market, because it virtually is any computer on the market, either PC or Mac.

Push on office programs so that you can really hire somebody who's not computer literate and they can still use it.
Mac OS 8, according to Dr. Amelio, will "enable average users—without the help of computer experts—to do things they never thought they could with a computer." (I may end up using my Mac for more than word processing after all.)

Have fewer models, and agree on a model.
The Power Mac is "fewer models" because it combines two different computers into one.

Create that kind of compatibility, where you bring us in your old processor and we'll turn it into a new one, because we don't want you to have to keep buying new computers.
On Apple's Web site, the company specifically states, "The Macintosh you buy today will run the next-generation Mac OS." (OS is short for Operating System, like Windows; it runs all your computer's software.)

IF A COMPUTER ILLITERATE LIKE ME COULD DO THAT, JUST IMAGINE WHAT YOU COULD DO

As you can see, not all my "hits" were right. The company doesn't seem interested in my beeper-apple idea, or in selling low-end products. And Apple seems to want to sell me more stuff rather than help me upgrade what I have. Quite possibly I had some intuitive interference. Again, I was not trying to predict what Apple *would* do, but rather what it *should* do to restore its own integrity with its market.

Intuition works even when you don't "know" much of anything about the subject you are investigating. Can you imagine how much clearer this intuitive reading would have been from someone familiar with the language of the computer market? Still, this reading demonstrates the power of intuition to suggest powerful improvements for any company—or you!

REVIEW YOUR PLAN AND MISSION STATEMENT FREQUENTLY

I need to reassess my goal in light of my progress. If I am experiencing difficulty or even failure, perhaps I am no longer in tune with my team or my market anymore.

~~~~~~

DAILY PRACTICE
MONITORING YOUR GOALS AND ENVIRONMENT

On a regular basis, spend a few moments to consider the following questions:

- In what ways has my situation changed?
- In what ways have my needs and priorities changed?
- In what ways has my environment changed?
- In what ways has my market changed?
- In what ways have the needs of my team changed?
- In what ways can I improve?
- In what ways do any of these affect each other?
- What kind of progress have I made toward these goals?

~~~~~~

~24~
Parting Words

This has been a book about using intuition in your business and career affairs. Business is not simply about "making a buck" or "getting ahead," but about satisfying your own needs by identifying and satisfying the needs of others.

Modern business practice seems to view everything in terms of beating the competition or competing effectively. This is a limiting viewpoint. In fact, if you find your niche—the market that wants what you have to offer—nobody can compete with you because nobody else has precisely what you have to offer.

Intuitive businesses and individuals succeed because they understand and respond to the simple fact, so often forgotten, that as people, companies, and products we need to work together to achieve our goals. We exist in a community, and our usefulness is only as enduring as the quality of our integrity within that community.

Intuition can help you find the information you need, both about yourself as well as your market, to make a difference and profit by being yourself.